Dedication Page

This book is dedicated to my Momma. She was eagerly anticipating its publication. I had her total support in my endeavor to document all of the things contained herein. She was thrilled and amazed each and every time I showed her new captures of bigfoot or told her about our encounters in the forest. She was my biggest fan and supporter.

Regretfully, she passed away before it was published. About 2 weeks before she passed, I completed writing it. She was very happy to hear that.

Though she will never get to physically hold it in her hand, I'm sure she knows my dream has finally become a reality. This book is for you Momma. I love you.

Dedication Page……………………………………............................1
Table of Contents…………………………………………2-3
Forward……………………………………………….4
Chapter 1- In the Beginning……………..……………5-10
Chapter 2- The Old House On Spruce Street………11-15
Chapter 3- The Big Black Mean Man……………….16-18
Chapter 4-The Haunting……………………………19-40
Chapter 5- Daddy……………………………………41-48
Chapter 6- Growing Pains…………………………..49-50
Chapter 7- Another Place and Time………………..51-54
Chapter 8- It Runs In The Family…………………..55-65
Chapter 9- Visitations………………………………66-72
Chapter 10- Mr. "Mann"……………………………73-79
Chapter 11- The Face Of Jesus……………………..80-82
Chapter 12- Evil Antiquities…………………………83-91
Chapter 13- Realizing The Impossible……………..92-95
Chapter 14- Bigfoot: The Introduction…………......96-99
Chapter 15- Gathering Evidence: Tree Structures………
……………………………………………..100-117
Chapter 16- Rocks, Rocks and More Rocks…….118-130
Chapter 17- Communication: Stick Glyphs……..131-155
Chapter 18- The Metting: Urijah and Family…...156-192
Chapter 19- Just Call Me Arocka………………..193-212

Chapter 20- The Gift of A Friend......................213-235

Chapter 21- My Friend Flute..........................236-242

Chapter 22- The Magic, Mystery and New Friendships Made at Stone Doll Holler...............................243-276

Chapter 23- The Warning on Terror Mountain...277-284

Chapter 24- Why Are They Always Blurry?.........285-287

Chapter 25- Close To Home............................288-310

Chapter 26- Seeing is Believing.......................311-325

Chapter 27- Various Captures.........................326-337

Chapter 28- Footprints In the Sand..................338-351

Acknowledgements......................................352-356

Copyright...357

Foreword

I have, for some time now, contemplated compiling some of my many life experiences and odd encounters into one condensed, self-contained book. This will be a daunting task as I have a great deal to share, but this is my attempt to do so. We will delve into the possibility of psychic connections, reincarnation, spirits, hauntings, past lives, visitations from deceased loved ones, ghosts, Bigfoot and their abilities, UFOs, and other cryptid creatures.

All I will be sharing with you is true and firsthand experiences. None of the subjects mentioned herein are "off limits" or taboo to me, being that all of these things I will share truly occurred and I have lived through each and every one of them. The truth will be told. Let's keep an open mind and not only think outside of the box. Let's just go ahead and throw that box away. Many things are possible when you let go of the mindset, we as a human race have been preprogrammed with from birth to accept as truth. Get rid of the "herd" mentality. Think for yourself. Not everything is black and white. You are only limited by your mind's boundaries and your willingness to accept things that may not rationally fit into that perfect box. Hence this book is being written.

So, I invite you to delve into this book with me and keep an open mind. I will provide you with an array of encounters that I have had as well as including some of those from various family members (with their permission). Names may or may not be changed to protect their privacy. Names of locations and/or historical figures will be omitted out of respect for any remaining family members and the privacy of those who call these areas home.

Chapter One

In The Beginning

Let me start at the very beginning. There have always been exceptionally strange and unusual events surrounding my existence. I have always been a person who has a "knowing", being very well aware of my existence before arriving on this planet we call Earth. I am an old soul occupying a new body. Before arriving here, I can, in vivid detail, remember where I was, who I was with and also being sent here to Earth, even though I objected profusely. I did not want to leave the beautiful place I was occupying. Never knowing that others did not have this ability, or had not had this experience, I assumed that this was normal for everyone and never spoke about it. Upon realizing that this was not the s"norm" for most people, I have been hesitant to speak about it...until now.

What do you call someone like me? I don't regard myself as "psychic". Am I a clairvoyant? Claircognizant? Intuitive? Is it precognition? Or am I a reincarnated soul or a visitor sent here with a mission? I tend to lean towards intuitive and the latter as well. I can only tell you that these things are so because they are my reality. I was raised by my father to believe that anything is possible. That if it looks like a duck, swims like a duck and quacks like a duck, it's a duck. I was never "brainwashed" with pre-conceived ideas to believe that certain things were not, or could not, be real or possible. I had, and still have, an open mind that believes anything is possible until proven 100% that it is not. So, I grew up with a very vivid reality of things that most people could not even imagine. After all, I saw, heard, and experienced it. And with a start to life like I had, I had no choice but to be open to it all.

As stated before, I have memories of the moments right before and after being born. Right before being born, I remember being in a very bright, beautiful place. There were trees that glistened and sparkled reflecting the light shining through the branches while the limbs gently swayed in the breeze. The trees lined a bank beside a glistening stream. The very air there sparkled and shone with vibrant colors. I remember walking hand in hand with a man there who was wearing a long white robe. He was an adult, and I was a child, and I was also wearing a clean, white robe. Looking up at Him as we walked, I can still vividly see His face in detail. He had shoulder length brown hair, a groomed beard, and bright blue eyes.

He didn't speak with His mouth. Rather just looking at me, I knew what He was "saying". He began to tell me I must go for now. There was something that I needed to do. I objected, not wanting to leave this paradise or Him because I loved Him so. On a side note, but also of extreme importance, since that time, being shown in great detail, I know who this was. You may or may not believe in Jesus, but that is who this was...and IS. I will explain this later on in another chapter dedicated exclusively to that crucial fact. Continuing with my conversation with Jesus, He sent me towards two other beings who stood beside a "box" that lay on the ground. Desperate to stay, I kept my eyes on the man who was speaking to me. Not paying much attention to these other two beings, I did not see their faces. But as He explained to me that He had something for me to do and that it was important for me to leave for a little while, the other two beings made me lay down inside of this "box". I saw their dark silhouettes as the light from above them shown from behind them. Appearing to be in human fashion but with very large wings on their backs. I thought to myself "This won't take long. I will be back before you know it" and grudgingly went along with what I was told I must do. The beings closed the top of the box by folding both sides of the top together as I was pushed out of the perfect world I was in. I watched as the bright light was shut out of sight. I was in total darkness.

A sketch I of what I saw as I lay in the box looking up. Silhouettes of 2 winged beings with an extremely bright light behind them.

Then in an instant, there was a "swooshing" and immediately I was in another place. It was like time and space were suspended here. It was very peaceful and quiet. I was suspended "floating" in my mother's womb. I liked it there. It was soothing and I thought to myself "This isn't so bad!" It doesn't seem like I was there but a few moments then "Swoosh!" again! I was being forced out of that peaceful place to a bright, cold room that didn't seem too inviting. I saw a man standing there reaching for me. I can see his face. He is smiling at me. I know this man. He will be my childhood doctor Mr. Wilson.

On a side note, this man brought me into this world by delivering me, then sent me out into the world, handing me my diploma as I graduated high school. What a coincidence...or maybe not. I don't much believe in coincidences.

As I was saying, he picked me up and handed me to a woman wearing a white dress and she abruptly swept me away wiping me off and cleaning me up as I screamed bloody murder. She apologized profusely as I screamed in pain after being poked with something sharp in my foot. She said "I'm so sorry! I know that hurt but I had to do it."

I did not like this new place. It was cold and way too bright with unfriendly, artificial lights. A far cry from the beautiful paradise I had been sent away from. But I had no choice in the matter. I was a helpless little baby. I was wrapped up in a blanket then laid down in a plastic bed on a cart. As I lay on my back, I saw the ugly, artificial, bright lights above me as I was wheeled around in this contraption up and down long hallways.

I saw a card above my head on this bed that read "McAnally Girl" How did I know what it said? I was an infant, but I was merely "occupying" this new, infant body. Why was I unable to get up and move around? Why did I have to rely on others to pick me up and move me around? I felt trapped inside the body I was now occupying. I did not like it.

The next thing I can recall is being at home with Momma holding me, caressing me gently as she told me how precious I was. This was nice! I thought to myself, "Now I can get used to this!"

Chapter Two

The Old House on Spruce Street

After coming home from the hospital, I have memories of living in the large, downstairs apartment that was my family's home at the time that I was born. Even though I was a baby, I clearly recollect the layout of the house. I later expressed to Momma about how I recalled all of this. I described everything unmistakably. She was astounded to say the least.

When I was 15 months old, my Daddy decided to purchase a home for us to call our own. There was an old grand, two-story house just around the corner from our apartment on the next block. It was for sale, and it was so big and spacious compared to our apartment. It had stately columns on the front porch and a lot of hand carved woodwork as the older homes do. It sat there as inviting as could be in all its splendor. The doors had (and still do to this day) wood carvings on them. Very decorative. There were frieze boards adorning the windows and doors. There was gingerbread and dentil trim placed at the peaks just below the roof's edge. It was beautiful!

This house was constructed in the 1880's. It was one of the first framed homes built in our town in that area. One day when I was a small child of about 5 years old, there came a knock on the front door. There stood two elderly women who were in their 70's. As we talked with them, they told us about growing up in the house. They told of how this was the only house in the area when they were children and how it was surrounded by dense woods. We later discovered, after some research, it was built and owned by the founder of our town.

He was a Union Army Captain. There are many stories circulating about him. As I did some research in the local library, I found others saying he was not a very nice man. He was not a friendly sort. He also owned slaves. There is a "slave shack" on the property behind the main house. In 1866, he set aside a 2-acre cemetery site up on a hill from his house on this property. Rumors abound that this cemetery was used for burying his former slaves. As the story goes, headstones were removed and used in construction of other buildings after the race riots in 1905 and 1909 forced all but one black resident from the county. We do not know if these rumors are true, however.

For one thing, cut stones would have been expensive, costing around $10 for a modest stone in the 1890's. That is the equivalent of several hundred dollars today. Most likely field stones would have been placed as markers for the graves, but with no carving to identify the one buried there. Some residents say they remember headstones marking graves in the cemetery. But others do not. All that remains there today is a sign in a vacant lot and a few remnants of broken stones scattered under a tree. It is a sort of no-man's land. There is no record of who is buried there, and no effort is being made to care for them. These poor souls are most likely at unrest up on the lonely hill, not being shown the respect they deserve. Sad to say, this was not abnormal for the way black people were treated back then. This sets the scene for some of the stranger things that are about to be experienced by my family in that old house as we moved in.

Photo taken of the house in the 1950's by a neighbor. Notice the "slave shack" behind the house.

This old house speaks to you. There is so much history contained inside these walls. There were many families who resided here and called it home over the 100+ years before we moved into it in May of 1969.

I distinctly remember the day we went to look at the house. Even though I was only 15 months old, it is as vivid in my mind today as it was then. It was such an exciting day! There were so many rooms and so much space for me and my sister to run and play. We were so excited to run free in the old empty house and explore as our parents talked with the sellers and negotiated a price for the sale of the house.

However, we were oblivious to the fact that there was something lurking upstairs. In a bedroom that was soon to be ours. As we explored and went into this room, I can remember our excitement. Then our terror. I was in front of my sister and ran into the room first. She was right behind me. As I entered the room, over against the far wall was a solid black figure. It was as dark as it could possibly be. As foreboding and nefarious as you can imagine. It was floating about two feet off of the floor. I saw a black trench coat and a black derby hat but there was no face where the face should have been. Only the hat floating above the coat. If you can, imagine an invisible man, and all you see are his clothes. This is what we saw.

As we entered the room and spotted this figure, it paused for a few seconds then flew with force through the wall facing the street. I spun around as I observed this, and my sister, who was right behind me, who also witnessed it, saw the terror in my eyes. She later told me my eyes were as big as saucers. This memory is so vivid in my mind. It is like it happened yesterday. And unfortunately, this was not the last time I would have a confrontation with this ominous figure.

Regardless of this occurrence, the house was now ours. We were to move in soon. My sister and I tried to dismiss the horrifying apparition that we had seen, trusting that it was probably gone for good. After all, it had flown outside through the wall. The excitement of having our own house and a big room all to ourselves outweighed the frightening experience. We had no idea what was to come. Little did we know, there was much more to come…much more.

Regardless, as we got used to our new home, it was a fun time. We had so much room to play, and it was all ours.

Chapter Three
The Big Black Mean Man

We had settled in and made the old house our new home. My sister and I had our own room. It was the master bedroom in the house. The largest room upstairs. It had two closets so we each had our own, and it was very spacious. My parents chose one of the other bedrooms upstairs that had one very large closet. The closet in their room gave access to the attic. Mine and my sister's room was always very cold for some unknown reason. There was a vent in the ceiling for the heat to come through but for some reason that no one could understand, it failed to get warm in that room. I remember sitting on that cold, hardwood floor so many times playing with my dolls. But we enjoyed having such a nice, big room all to ourselves.

Then, there came a day that I cannot ever forget. It is as vivid today as the day it happened to me. I was an innocent 4-year-old child. My Momma, sister and I were downstairs watching The Price Is Right. We loved that show and never missed an episode! Like clockwork, at 10 a.m., the television was switched to channel 10 for our favorite mid-morning entertainment. I remember Momma had a basket of warm clothes fresh out of the dryer and was folding them. I wanted to go upstairs to my room to get my favorite Barbie doll. So, I ventured up the stairs and made my way to my room. As I entered the doorway, there in front of the far wall once again, was the big black trench coat and hat floating in midair. The hat was almost to the ceiling and the coat was about 2 feet above the floor. It was just as my sister and I had seen the day we went with my parents to purchase the house. I immediately stopped in terror at the doorway. I hesitate to use the word "apparition" here because this figure was as solid as you and I. It was not ghostly or transparent in any way, shape, or form. But, on this day, this ominous, solid black figure began to fly towards me! It flew through the air, swooping back and forth to the right and then to the left. It cackled wildly as it got closer and closer to me. The evil laughing that it exuded was horrifying. I was terrified! It was back, and this time it is coming after me! I spun around and ran as hard as I could to get back to the stairs. I kept looking over my shoulder and all I could see was this black figure swooping back and forth right behind me. I felt impending doom was forthcoming and I was not going to make it out of there alive.

I don't know how I managed to navigate down those stairs without falling and breaking my neck. But somehow, I eventually reached the bottom. I scampered to my Momma's side who was still folding the clothes and wailed at the top of my lungs "Big black mean man!" I shrieked adamantly that there was someone or something upstairs and it was going to hurt me. I knew I was going to suffer, and I knew it was going to be in a most painful way.

My Momma was incredulous and a very rational person. She was a loving, nurturing mother and took wonderful care of my sister and me. But, at least at that point and time, she absolutely refused to believe in anything that she could not explain away in a logical manner. Or, at least, she wanted to portray that normalcy for us as kids so we wouldn't get carried away and scared of everything that went bump in the night.

I watched in trepidation as she wandered up those stairs just knowing she would be horrified when she saw what was lurking upstairs. But instead, she simply told me, no if's, and's or but's about it, that there was absolutely nothing there. Period. End of discussion. I insisted that the big black mean man was going to hurt me. She was clueless to the terror I had just experienced.

From that day forward, at least until later in life, I realized telling her about anything that happened to me or anything that I saw would be taken with a grain of salt and explained away. There was no such thing as the big black mean man or anything closely resembling him. But I kept all these things in my heart. I KNEW with certainty that he was there and that there was something inexplainable going on.

I later learned that my Daddy also had these types of experiences. He didn't reveal this to me until I was older because he was afraid it would frighten me.

So, I continued on, terrorized by all that was happening to me and not being able to talk about it with anyone. After all, these things do not exist.

Or do they?

Chapter Four
The Haunting

My entire existence up until this day has been nothing but paranormal and odd encounters. I have never known a life of what other people would call "normal". In my experience, there has never been a shortage of odd or strange encounters. There is no way I could possibly include all of the experiences we each had in this house. No book could contain it all. I am sharing just a scant few in this chapter.

As we got settled into our new home, there were so many baffling, unexplainable things happening. Numerous times, when we fell asleep upstairs in our bedrooms, Daddy would hear what he suspected to be burglar's downstairs. Oftentimes, the pots and pans in the kitchen would make such a clamor as to wake us up. Kitchen cabinets were opening and slamming shut loudly, and much commotion was going on. At times, it would sound as if there was a big celebration going on downstairs as we lay in our beds trying to sleep upstairs. Piano music playing, and a lot of people talking and laughing. Daddy would creep down the stairs, reach around the corner to flip on the light, then jump out into the middle of the room, hammer in hand, ready to teach the "intruders" a lesson. There was never a soul in sight. Yet, often we heard the ruckus going on downstairs as we tried to sleep.

On a side note, Momma told me that the woman who had resided there sometime prior to us, taught piano lessons. Was this a residual haunting like a movie that replays over and over, lost somewhere in time? Was she entertaining her party guests by tickling the ivories as she did many years ago? Or was she simply returning once again to play the piano for us to enjoy?

And this was only the beginning. There were many more years of unexplainable and disturbing things to come. All these things were experienced by myself, my sister, friends that were visiting at times and Daddy.

Daddy got the brunt of it. He was intuitive as I am. He "saw" things that others did not. When I was a child, he did not speak about any of the things he experienced for fear of frightening my sister and I. Little did he know, we were having some of the same experiences and we were already terrified. I wish he had spoken to me about it when I was younger because I had no idea why these things were happening and WHAT was happening. But when I was older, he began to share some of these things.

He told me in later years that he had many visitors to his room. He told me that many times, he would be lying in bed and observe two small girls dressed in white 1800's style dresses. They were holding hands, spinning around and around in circles laughing and singing ring around the rosie at the foot of his bed. He also told of a misty figure of a woman standing beside his bed one night. As he reached to touch her, she fell into the floor like sand sifting down through an hourglass until she completely vanished.

Another time as he was sleeping, he was awakened by something sitting on his chest chattering wildly. He explained this as sounding similar to an old cassette tape recording on fast forward and what he was hearing was incomprehensible. He immediately said, "Get away from me Satan!" He watched in terror as it flew through the room and out of a closed window, causing the curtain to fly up into the air as it abruptly exited his room.

Daddy had another frequent visitor to his bedside whom he was not fond of. This was a gruff, old man in overalls. He had a long white beard and would wake him up telling him "Get up! Get out of bed! It's time to go!" He would shake him trying to rouse him out of bed. Daddy got so frustrated with this spirit. And there were many more phenomenon transpiring and happening to him.

He would hear footsteps on the hard wood floors (as I did). It sounded like boots walking across the floor. Oftentimes, while home alone, he would suddenly hear walloping on the front door. Then it would quickly travel all the way around the entire perimeter of the house, beating on each and every window as it went. There is no way that anything or anyone could have traveled this fast. The family dog would bark wildly and run blindly around the house trying to find what was making all of this thunderous noise. Nothing was ever found. There was no one outside and no one was ever seen. Beside the point that the quickness of the banging on each window and door was not humanly possible.

The family also had a cat at one time. Her name was Tinker. She lived her entire life there and died there. After her passing, Daddy was lying in bed. He felt the familiar jump on the bed and her gentle steps as she walked across the covers, making herself comfortable and lying down beside him.

There was also another time when I was visiting him. As he walked through his bedroom door, he watched as his large reclining chair quickly slid across the floor and was wedged itself up against his bookshelf. This happened in the middle of the day, and I was there to hear it hit the bookshelf. I witnessed where the chair was when it landed. What just happened? How did this large, heavy chair slide on its own across the floor with such force?

The next two pages here are excerpts from daddy's book of letters and stories he had written. These are the actual pages taken out of it. He wanted to chronicle things that had happened to him and also about his life and his Lord. He was quite the writer. He had some trouble spelling, but his way of wording things was beautiful. He was a very eloquent author. These two are fitting for this chapter…

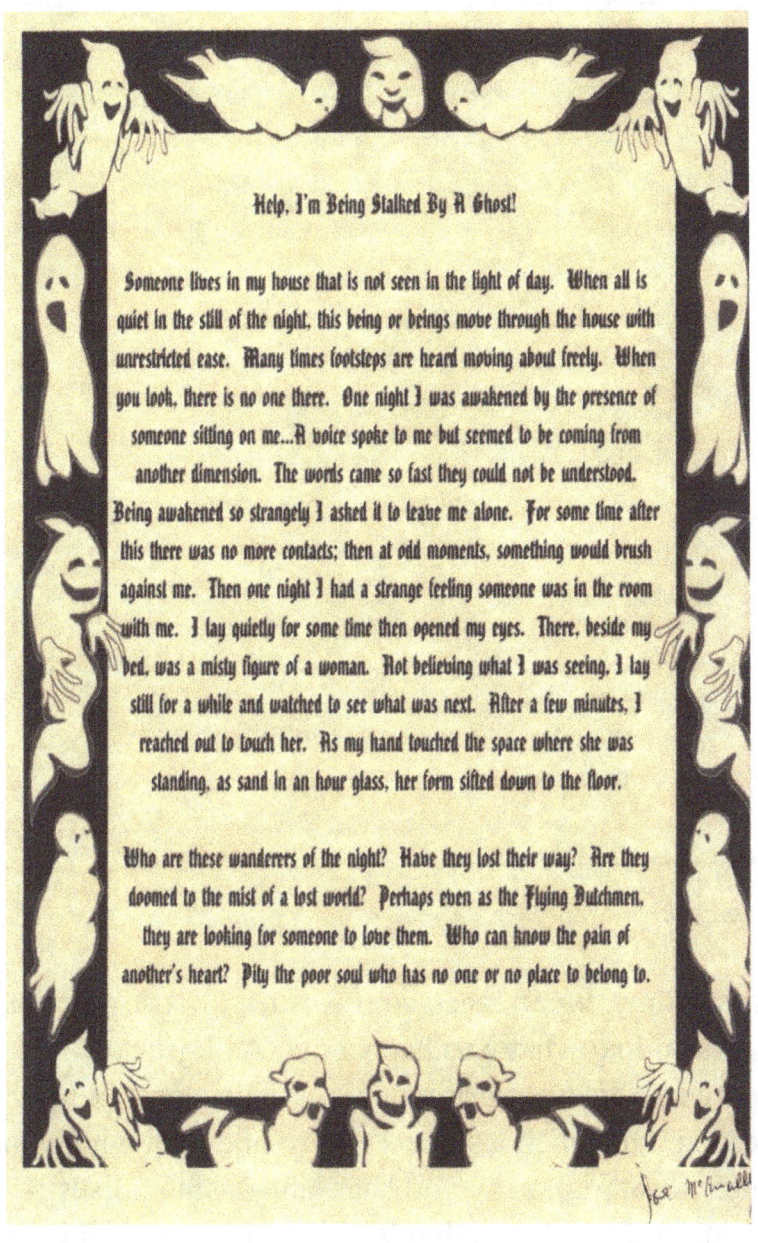

Page in Daddys book about the ghosts he encountered.

Page from Daddys Book of stories about Tinker the cat

```
                            TINKER
     Tinker was the name we gave the little black kitten that came looking
     for a home. She was about as big as a, well, as a baby kitten.
     She lived in the house because she was to little to take care of herself
     out side. This soon begain to cause a problem. There was the litter box,
     there was the water dish, there was the food dish, then she had to have
     kitten food. As she grew larger I desided she had to go out of the house.
     Tinker did not agree with me on this at all. Her favrite place to sleep
     was in the center of the bed and she was not about to give that up with
     out a fight. After many battles she did give in for the warm nights of
     sumer but she did come in, in the winter cold, because her bed out side
     was just not warm enough.
     This arangement went on for the following years. Tinker was always very
     loveing. She seemed to thank us for her home and family.
     Then one morning in May we found her body laying as though she were
     sleeping.
     I gathered her body into a water proof plastic bag and layed her to rest
     under the large pine tree she loved to lay under on a hot day.
     I though, that is the last time Tinker will sleep in my bed. That night
     I went to bed, very tired thinking of the past day, looking forward to
     a good nights sleep. Having lived with strange things happening in the
     night for the past 30 years I was not bothered when I felt movement at
     the foot of my bed. As I lay quitely waiting for the activityactivity to
     settel down, suddenly a very familiar movemet begin, one which it I had
     felt many times. No it cannot be . Tinker had come to spend one more
     night on my bed.
     The way she moved across the bed , picking her feet up as though she were
     walking in water, no other movement ever matched the foot steps of Tinker.
     Did she come back to bid me farewell? To let me know she is all right?
     Or will she join the others who have visited my bed these past years?

     THIS WAS DIFFERENT FROM THE REST IN THAT THIS WAS ONE WHO I HAD KNOWN
     I LAY QUIELY NOT WANTING TO BREAK THE MAGIC OF THE MOMENT. SHE APERANTLY
     ONLY WANTED TO SAY GOOD BYE. SHE HAS NOT RETURNED SENCE THAT NIGHT.

         FARE WELL TINKER, MAY YOUR NEW HOME ALWAYS BE A HAPPY PLACE.
```

As far as my experiences go, I was terror-stricken, not understanding what was happening. As I grew, I experienced many alarming things. The closet in my bedroom contained a sinister figure of a man who would watch me at night. I would hear hair-raising noises coming from underneath my bed. Many times, as I slept, my ankles would be grabbed, and I was unable to move. I was yanked out of bed and pulled under the bed as I lay there on the cold, hardwood floor in terror. I didn't understand what was happening. But I did know Momma would not believe me. I lay there screaming many nights, crying for someone to help me. My sister seemed to sleep through it all. Sometimes she would yell at me to shut up. I don't understand how she could sleep with me crying at the top of my lungs. And this continued for years…

I would see ghostly fog moving through the house at times. I saw orbs of light flying through the house and sometimes through the walls. At times, I saw what appeared to be sparkling lights, reminding me of a sparkler on the 4th of July. They would simply filter through the ceiling. Voices could be heard calling my name or sometimes just muffled talking. They still do this to this day. My daughter heard my name called loudly from a corner of the room about a month ago while visiting Momma.

One day, later on in life, after I had already moved out and had children of my own, I decided to set up an audio recorder. This was before all the modern technology. We used an old tape recorder with a cassette tape. I set the recorder in my old bedroom. The same room I used as a child. The same room my sister and I had seen the "big black mean man". I turned it on to record right before my son Clayton and I had to leave for a doctor's visit. No one was home. I pressed the record button not knowing what we would capture or if we would capture anything at all. When we returned about 2 hours later, I turned the recorder off. I took the cassette home and listened intently a little at a time, because after all, it was around 2 hours long.

At first, I heard little noises as if someone was tapping on the recorder to see what it was and why it was there. Thump! Thump! It then progressed to voices talking in the room. I heard a young girl's voice saying, "Happy Birthday...MIA!" Mia was my Momma's dog. Then I heard two girls giggling and laughing. Then there was the sound of a very loud truck going down the street outside. After that, the little girl's voices saying "Did you hear that truck? Did you hear it? Did you hear it" then giggling again. Oddly the voices of the young girls sounded like my own voice. Are they mimicking my voice? If so, why?

These two girls have been witnessed by my Daddy, myself and even my husband Eric. Eric witnessed one of them as she stood in an upstairs window looking down at him as he stood outside. She was seemingly lost in time. My daughter Amber, at one time, occupied a bedroom in the house as well. She told of noises of children talking and giggling at night while she was trying to go to sleep.

I, at one time, also observed the apparition of a young boy in the house as well. He was dressed in knickers and a newsboy cap. He stood motionless, holding a box in his hands, against his chest out in front of him. As I looked at this misty form standing there, I blinked, and he was no longer there. This boy and these girls seem to play together because we hear their voices often as they laugh and seem to be having such great fun.

My husband Eric witnessed this firsthand as he was at the house working on Momma's broken washing machine one day. We had all left the house leaving Eric there alone. As he lay on the floor working on the washer, he heard kids' laughter and talking directly behind him. He rose up to look around and saw no one. As he returned to work on the washer, he again heard them. He abruptly got up and went outside. When we returned, he was outside waiting for us. We asked him why he wasn't inside finishing his repair job. He refused to go back into that house alone. He was very shaken up about it.

Again, another time these children were heard and recorded. I brought my video camera over, and I sat it up in my old bedroom upstairs. We left the house so there would be no other noises inside polluting the video. After retrieving the camera, we anxiously watched what was recorded to see if we could see or hear anything.

The camera was slightly bumped or jarred at one point. Then it was violently jerked to the side. We heard an unusually loud, boisterous noise of what you would hear if a child, with a stick in hand, ran alongside a rail with balusters, hitting each one with the stick as he was dragging it across them. This went on and on. Back and forth, back and forth. We heard the voice of a little boy. Then we heard the girls giggling and speaking to the boy. It sounded as if they were having great fun. Then, suddenly, we heard a very deep, gruff man's voice. It was not a friendly voice at all. He was chastising these children. The children immediately stopped playing and talking.

There was then a thunderous, deafening noise. I can only explain it as sounding as if an airplane was taking off INSIDE THE ROOM! It was deafening. The camera began to shake and bounce around wildly as the noise reverberated throughout the entire room. After about 20 seconds of this, it all went completely silent, and the camera came to a standstill. Everything simply stopped abruptly. What in the world was happening? What did we just witness?

Again, I set up the camera another day, focusing it this time in the room my Daddy used which was downstairs directly under my room. We exited the house and left it filming to see if anything at all would happen. When we returned and reviewed what had been filmed while we were away, we were shocked. We saw an orb of light flying through the room. It seemed to have a mind of its own as its flight pattern was very specific and intelligent. It followed the top of the wall and went around each window. It maneuvered around items in the room. Then it flew out of view.

Then the phone began relentlessly ringing. It would ring as many as 15 times each time then it would hang up. Immediately, it would begin ringing again. It continuously did this for around ten minutes. There were no missed calls on the caller id and no messages were left. Then we heard what sounded like a large group of people singing. As we listened to it, Momma exclaimed, "That sounds like a choir!" And it did! There was absolutely no one there and it should have been basically silent apart from any random car noise as it traveled along the street. We still have no explanation for this occurrence. The same way we have none for anything else that we have witnessed there.

On a side note, the phone ringing has happened many times to all of us. And still does to this day. The phone will ring, and the caller id shows it is Momma's own number calling. It shows my Daddy's name as the caller. When you answer it, it is silent. There is no one there.

Objects get moved about frequently in the house as well. Sometimes, they completely vanish, then are returned at a later time. I remember as a teenager, looking for a specific shirt or something to wear. I would search piece by piece through every article of clothing hanging in my closet. I was unable to find it. I would become so frustrated and even search diligently through every article of clothing hanging in Momma's closet. Whatever that particular item of clothing would be that I was searching for was nowhere to be found. I would ask Momma if she knew where it was, but she was clueless because all our clothes had been freshly laundered and were hanging in the closets. Occasionally, the following day, or maybe even two or three days later, I would see that particular shirt or whatever hanging there in my closet in plain view. This also happened to Momma as well. She would get so irritated, come to my room, and question me, asking if I had borrowed one of her tops. I had not but she searched through my closet nevertheless not finding what she was looking for. This always happened to me with my belt. I ALWAYS left my belt on a chair in my room. It would simply vanish for a few days then be returned to the chair where I had looked intently for it previously.

Recently, Momma "lost" her magnifying glass. It always sat there on the kitchen cabinet beside the cookie jar. That was "its place". She searched but could not find it. We scoured the entire house looking for it. A few days later it appeared there in the exact spot it was always kept…right beside the cookie jar.

My son, Clayton, at one time had his own room at the old house too. He used my old bedroom. One day he lost his wallet. It contained all of his important belongings including his driver's license and his social security card. He knew that he had left it on his desk in his room. We searched and searched. It was nowhere to be found. About a week later, he went into his room and there on his desk sat his wallet where he always kept it. So very strange.

Another time, a couple of days before Thanksgiving, everything on one of the walls in Daddy's bedroom was disheveled. Every picture hanging on that wall was either turned sideways or on the floor. The flag that was contained in a flag case from his funeral was there on the wood box having been knocked off the wall as well. He had a pin of an airplane that was a replica of one of the planes he worked on in the Navy during WW2 hanging on the wall. It was in a plastic case. The case was found broken and lying on the floor. But the pin was nowhere to be found. We combed that room over and over trying to find that airplane pin. It was not there. Then, a couple of days before Thanksgiving the following year, one year to the date, there sat that airplane pin on top of the tv in his room. Momma had dusted this tv probably a hundred times in that year and it was not there. We all knew it was not there because we had all examined his room from top to bottom, searching for that pin.

These are just a few examples of occurrences. There were many more. Where do these things go when they disappear and why are they taken? How can something be taken away and hidden for a period of time then returned to the exact spot where they were last seen? I do not understand this at all.

Then, there are photos that are taken with unexplainable things being present in them. We took a photo on Christmas of 1996. There appeared to be someone or something peeking out of the window upstairs. You can clearly see a face and what appears to be a hand pressed

Photo taken in 1996 on the front porch. Certain individuals

blacked out for privacy. Daddy (far left) Momma and me. Sitting is my son Clayton and daughter Amber.

up against the window. This window is in my old bedroom where most of the odd occurrences happened.

Zoomed in and lightened up you can see a face peering through the left windowpane with a hand pressed against it.

Eyes dotted by me for reference.

There was another time a few years back that my daughter Amber and I ventured into my old bedroom to take photos. We enjoyed doing this because we were like detectives, trying to piece this puzzle together, and we occasionally captured something in our photos.

On this particular day, I stood in the doorway taking photos towards the inside of the room. Amber was standing in the other room behind me. As I snapped 3 photos in the direction of the dresser mirror, I captured something that was unseen by us at the time.

In the first photo, there is nothing there. In the second photo, something began to appear. On the bottom right side, there appears to be something that looks sort of like a troll wearing a reddish colored shirt standing in front of me. There is also a weird puff of what looks like ectoplasm beside him. He appears to be turned a bit to the side. On the left upper side of the same photo, there is "something" that appears to be coming through the wall. In the third photo, you can see the "troll" is now facing forward. There is now also an arm protruding through the wall of the the closet, reaching towards this little being on the floor. Where the arm goes through the wall is a bright light. You can clearly see the hand and its fingers spread apart as if desperately trying to reach this little troll being. Whoever this is, is wearing a reddish colored shirt as you can see the sleeve! What is this? Is this little troll the same one I captured in the photograph taken on the front porch back in 1996?

There is nothing there in the first photo. This is the dresser mirror.

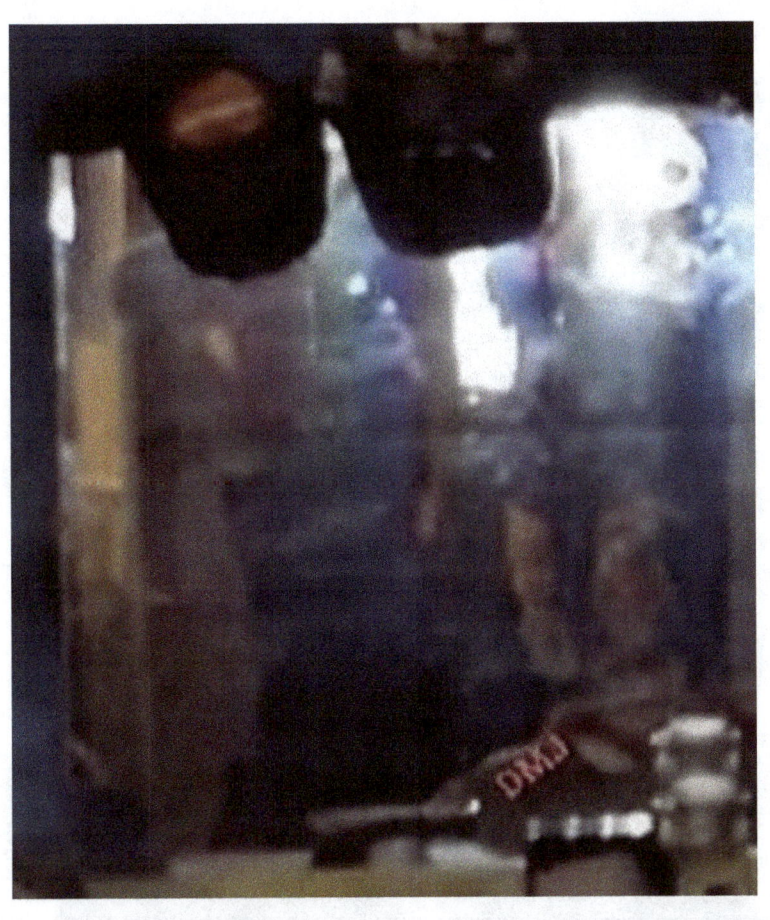

Here, you can start to see the figure on the bottom right side of the photo. On the upper left side, you can begin to see "something" coming through the wall.

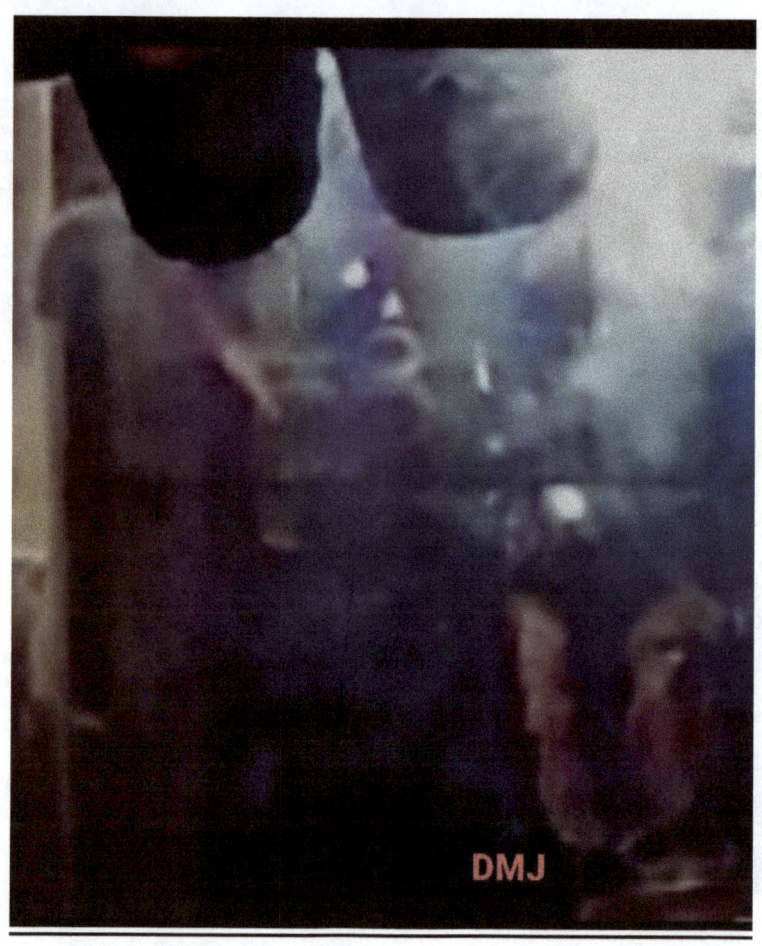

In this 3rd photo, you can now clearly see the "troll" being standing on the right bottom with what appears to be a fog of ectoplasm or something beside him. The arm is also now visible on the upper left side with outstretched fingers reaching towards this little troll being as it comes through the wall.

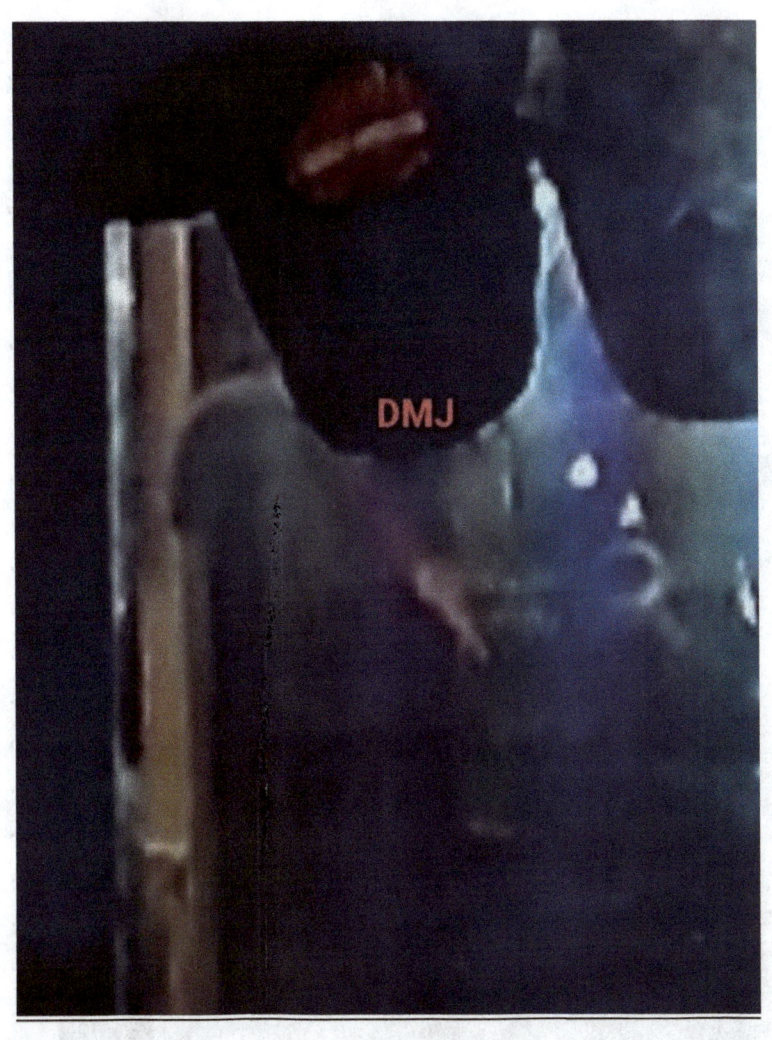

<u>Here is a close up of the arm reaching through the wall. Notice the red sleeve and outstretched fingers!</u>

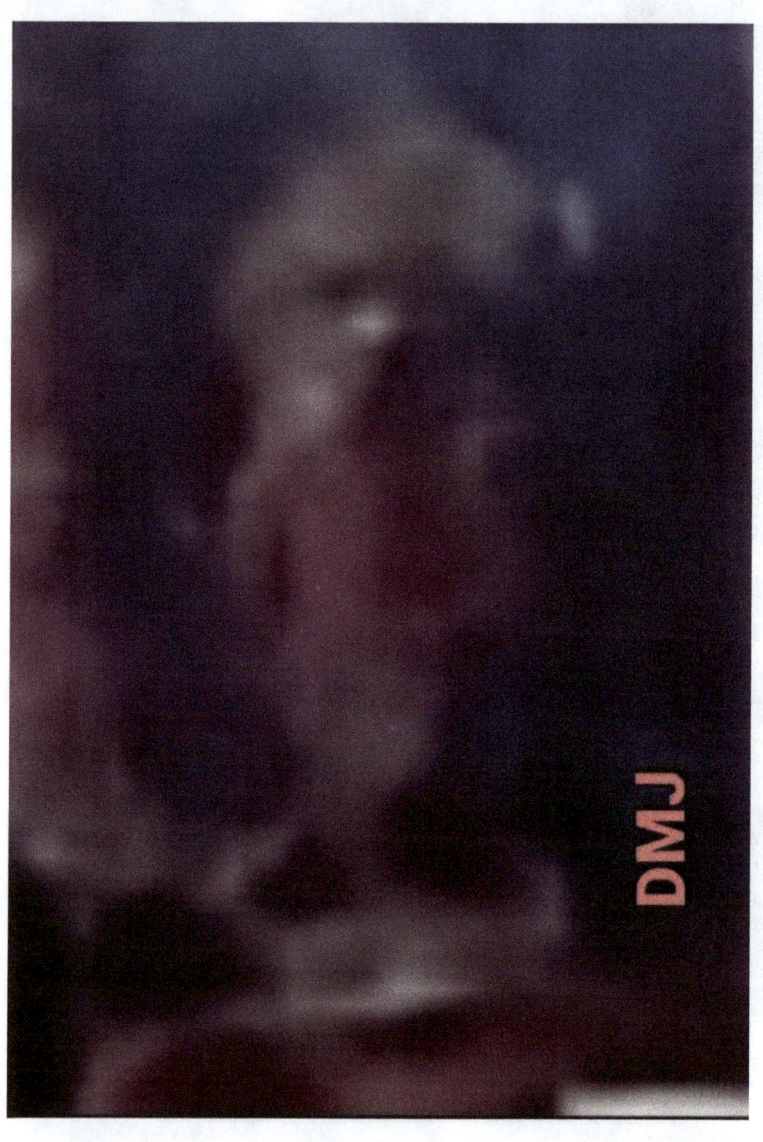

Close up of the "troll" You can see his face and he appears to be wearing a reddish colored shirt.

Eyes dotted by me for reference.

Who or what is this being? I call him a troll because that is what he looks like to me. And who is reaching through a solid wall for him? This makes absolutely no sense to me. I could accept the fact that a ghost or the spirit of a person who has passed over might be here. But this thing is not human. This borders on some type of spiritual warfare.

Ephesians 6:12 reads "For we wrestle not against flesh and blood, but against principalities, against powers, against the rulers of the darkness of this world, against spiritual wickedness in high places."

I do not like this non-human apparition showing up in my photos. I do not like it at all.

Chapter Five

Daddy

"It"

It was cold one dark night, not long after Christmas. In a cabin in the hills so far from anywhere, seldom was anyone ever seen, a frail little creature was about to make his entrance into the world. After what seemed a long time, there came the wail of one who did not like the world to which he was being born into. His mother asked dad, "What is it?" His dad said, "I don't know, but if you want it, keep it hid until it looks like something. As for me, I'm going fox hunting." Mother said, "I suppose we will have to keep it. Maybe if we let it outside it will wander off and get lost, or some animal will carry it off."

No such luck, "It" could run like a deer, climb like a squirrel, and pop the head off a snake. Mother told everyone it had been sent to her from Africa. Dad pretended "It" was not there, hoping no one would notice it.

After a few years, "It" stopped causing so much of a problem, and even became accepted in the neighborhood. "It" sure is not much to look at, but is kinda handy to have around. Will someone go to the mailbox? Send "It", he is faster than anyone else; anyway, he likes to do things, it makes him feel like he is one of the kids.

Who am I? My name is written on the wind.

"It"

Page from Daddy's book of writings

My Daddy was a very interesting man to say the least. He was born in 1922 and lived through the great depression. He told me stories of how he lived in the big woods as a child. The big holler was his playground. They lived 12 miles out in the woods. He said there were not any roads to where they lived. You had to use a horse and buggy to get to their home. He had much to say about how they lived and things he did as a child.

He grew up in a family who was struggling. The great depression had everyone struggling. There was very little money. No one could find work to buy food. Their clothes were worn out. The food his mother had canned and put in the food cellar was about to run out. They prayed for rain so some food would grow. God answered their prayer but not in a way they expected.

Daddy. Small blonde child on right with his parents and brothers

A friend asked daddy if he would like to make some money. He could hardly believe his ears. "I sure would!" he replied. The father of this friend of his had some timber on his land that he didn't need, so if they cleaned up the brush, they could cut and sell the timber for stove wood to people who lived in town.

Everyone in the family had to do their part. When he was only around 5 years old, his daddy told him he needed to get a job, or "he wasn't aiming to take care of him."

Daddy asked a man who had a strawberry patch if he could get a job picking strawberries, so his daddy wouldn't kick him out of the house. He got the job and made enough money to buy his books and supplies and pay his expenses for the next school year so, his daddy let him stay. He made a dime a day. This was a lot of money back then during the great depression.

Class photo circa 1930. Red arrow points to Daddy.

Another job Daddy and his brother Henry had was working the hay field. Henry was cutting sprouts for 50 cents a day. Daddy made $1.25 a day in the hay field and got to eat lunch with the crew. Then along came Fady Scarborough. This guy said he would work for 35 cents a day cutting sprouts and bring his own lunch. My Daddy and his brother got fired and Fady took their place. They decided to put a scare into this guy. They made up a story about a panther in the woods who was attacking folks. Then, they hid in the woods as this other fellow walked along the dark path on his way home carrying a shotgun for protection. It was after dark, and they howled out to scare the guy. This guy took off running and ended up shooting a poor little dog. He told everyone the next day that he had killed that panther.

Sadly, growing up, Daddy was not treated very well. He said that his mother had her favorite child, and his father had his favorite child, and he was just in the way. As I talked about earlier, as a 5-year-old child, he was going to be kicked out of the house if he couldn't get a job, so he learned to take care of himself very early on. He told me that his father was a very blunt man. He would not tell a lie to save his own neck. He simply said it as it was or at least what was on his mind. He had no filter. One day, when Daddy was older, he said his father told him "I bet you have always wondered why we treat you the way we do. Well, the simple fact of the matter is that we didn't want you." What a horrible thing to tell someone, especially your own child.

I never got to meet my grandfather and maybe it was for the best. I don't really appreciate the way Daddy was treated as a child. Later in life as a young adult, he and his father did things together like working on cars and building the house that they lived in, and his father finally accepted him as a person. He now had something useful (in his father's eyes) to offer. Nevertheless, Daddy still respected his father and took care of him during his last years driving him to the doctor's office and such. I don't think I would have been so strong or eager to help a person who told me that I was never wanted. Because of the way Daddy was treated as a child by his own father, he made sure I felt loved as a child and made sure I felt like an important part of the family. He always treated me with love. He also treated each of his grandchildren the same way. You shouldn't have to earn someone's love. He made sure we all knew we were an important part of the family. That we mattered and each of us had something valuable to contribute.

Even though he was treated as an outcast by his immediate family, he told me of his grandpa who assured him that he was valuable. He treated him with respect and taught him most of the morals he carried with him throughout his life. This was Henry, my grandmother's father, whom he loved dearly. Thank God for Grandpa Henry. He walked with 2 walking sticks everywhere he went. Daddy would walk with him and keep him company as he went. He said if grandpa had needed something or had needed help as they walked, at least he could have run to get someone to help. So, he always walked with him everywhere he went. As they walked and talked, Grandpa Henry would stop occasionally and sit down for a rest. He would read the bible to my daddy and teach him the way he should live. These values were instilled in Daddy at a very young age, and he carried it with him throughout his life. He also instilled these values into each of his children and grandchildren. I thank God for Grandpa Henry.

A **Photo of Grandpa Henry. Notice the 2 walking sticks.**

After surviving his difficult childhood and growing into a young adult, WW2 started. Daddy went into the Navy. They needed mechanics to keep the airplanes flying. He signed up for the training school and they accepted him. He thanked God for his new job. It was a good life. He had plenty of good food, good clothes, and a good house to live in. He said he grew into manhood in the Navy and again God gave him more than he had hoped for. He had a purpose. He was very good at what he did, and he was much needed. So much so, they never let him go out to sea, much to his dismay.

Daddy second from right in front of an F6F airplane that he worked on during WW2.

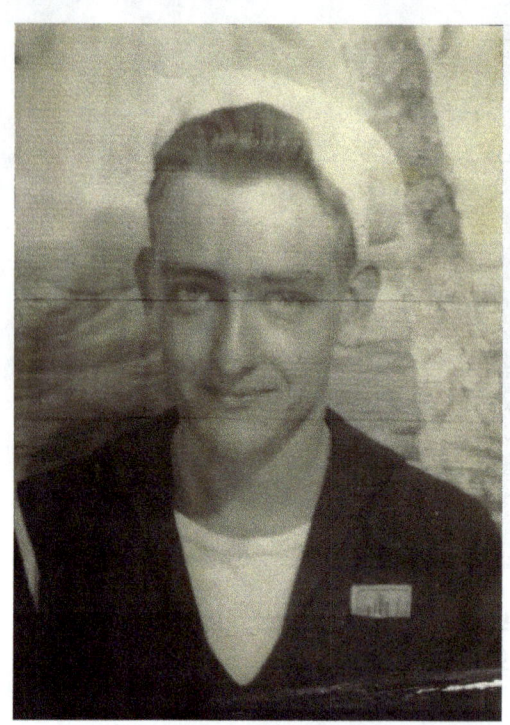

Notice the paycheck in his pocket.

Chapter Six
Growing pains

As I stated before, the paranormal was always as vivid to me as reality. It WAS my reality, and I had a hard time discerning the two. As children, we played many games. Back in the 1970's, the big thing was The Ouija Board "game" by The Parker Brothers. Funny to say that Momma who didn't believe in anything paranormal (at that time) purchased my sister and I one to play with. Back then it was considered a game and that's what it was advertised as. I suppose because it was in the toy section at the store.

My sister and I would ask it questions and sit there on the edge of our seats as the planchette would slowly creep across the board to reveal answers. It was fun and entertainment for us. Though we didn't realize how it worked or what was making the planchette move.

My sister was quite a bit older than me, and she was always showing our friends and I new and fascinating things. You must understand that back in the 1970's, dabbling in and participating in "seances" and things like that was a normal thing for kids to do. At least that was the reality that was introduced to me by my older sister. It was our entertainment. We found that the "light as a feather, stiff as a board" played by children back then, really did work! Each child put two fingers under a person laying on the floor and after chanting "light as a feather, stiff as a board" over and over, that person would begin to float! My niece Teresa and nephew David along with some neighborhood friends played this many times. This is how we entertained ourselves. My sister always introduced new things like this to amuse us and it gave us something exciting to do.

Did all of this childish game play open another door? Or was the door already open? I knew there was already something formidable going on, but did we make it worse?

One time, I can remember playing with the Ouija board as me and a friend who was spending the night with me asked it questions. Suddenly, we heard a thunderous crash as the neighbor's trash cans seemed to be violently thrown to the pavement and rolled down the street. Then, out of the blue, the message we received from the Ouija board was "big black bug downstairs". We reluctantly went down the stairs and flipped the light on. There in the middle of the room was a big black bug of some sort! We screamed in terror and ran back up the stairs to the "safety" of my room. But when we got there, we saw what appeared to be a gigantic handprint on the dresser mirror. It was so frightening to us that we put the Ouija board away and we didn't play with it anymore. That was enough!

Chapter Seven
Another Place and Time

As a child, I had a recurring dream. I had this dream regularly, at least two times a week over all the years that I lived in my childhood home. It was always the same. This dream started with two other children and me. We were dressed in clothing that seemed appropriate for the 1800's. Attire you would see on Little House on The Prairie. I wore a dress and bloomers. There was one other girl there and we both had braids in our hair. There was also a boy with us who wore knickers and a newsboy cap.

In this dream, we were in a large field of flowing, tall, yellow grass swaying in the breeze. In the middle of this field was a boardwalk. This did not make sense to me. Why would a boardwalk be out in the middle of this field of tall swaying grass? The wood was weathered and discolored showing its age. I'd say it was about 4 feet wide. As we stood on this boardwalk in the middle of this field, we looked up to the top of a hill and there alone stood a menacing two story, white clapboard house. Nothing else was there. No trees or anything else. It appeared that the paint was peeling on the old house. The boardwalk made its way all the way up the hill to the old house. I and the other two children walked the long pathway on the old boardwalk to reach the house. For some reason, it was rather frightening as we stepped onto the porch. Literally, in all the hundreds of times I have had this exact same dream, we NEVER made it inside that old house. Reaching that porch is where I woke every time. And I never told a soul about this dream. Now that is odd enough in itself. But wait, there is more…

One day my daughter Amber was talking to me about a dream she had many times while she was also living in my childhood home. She told me about this experience after she was grown and she had children of her own. She started explaining to me the familiar scene that I had seen so many times in my own dream. I immediately stopped her. I asked her for explicit details about the dream. She explained in detail to me the same things I had dreamed about as a child! The absurd, unexplainable boardwalk that went through the middle of a field of tall, swaying, yellow grass. The other two children and the clothing they all were wearing. The menacing, big two-story white house sitting at the top of the hill. How did she know about these things? These were my secret thoughts and my dreams, and she knew every detail. But both of us only had this dream while living in the old house on Spruce Street. After moving from the premises, neither of us ever had that dream again.

How did my daughter and I have this same recurring dream? Was this some sort of message to both of us or was this dream actually an experience we both had from another lifetime? Were her and I the two girls in the dream? To this day, we have not figured it out, but it seems to go hand in hand with all the strangeness that comes along with the house.

As long as I am going down the rabbit hole so to speak, speaking about possible psychic connections and possible past lives, I will tell you that my experiences do not end at that one recurring, shared dream with my daughter. When does our conscience being, our existence as we know it, begin or end?

I have a granddaughter by my daughter Amber. Her name is Aubree. One day, when she was only four years old, we were shopping, and she suddenly looked at me and asked me if I remembered playing with her when we were both babies. She told me that we had so much fun together and insisted that I should remember this. I asked her who our Mommy was, and she said "Grandma". A few days earlier I showed her where I used to live before we moved to the house she now knows as Grandmas house on Spruce Street. Consequently, it was also a white house. She exclaimed "Oh I remember that place!"

I lived there as a baby 44 years before she was born…

Again, at four years old, Aubree tried explaining to my daughter Amber about a white house Grandma used to live in. Did my showing her the other house jar her memory? She seems to have memories of her and I together in a white house from beyond this present place and time and we were the same age. She says we played tag and hide and seek. I was not her Ma Ma at the time. Then she said "We laid down and we went to sleep. We did not wake up anymore. And that is all."

This may be a long shot, but my Momma was pregnant with twins before I was born. My Daddy told me about this and that they were girls almost fully formed when they lost their lives during a miscarriage. Momma was about 4 months along.

Could this have been Aubree and me? Is this a true memory of hers or just a story she has made up in her mind? Maybe this is simply a dream she has had. There is also a chance that it may be absolutely nothing. We may never know. Life is full of mysteries and unexplainable things. Someday it will all be revealed to us, and we will understand everything. Including the meaning and purpose of our lives.

Again, about a month later, Aubree asked me about playing with a specific toy with my son Clayton in the front yard of Mommas house. She told me that she remembered doing this. She explained to me in detail what the toy was that we were playing with. It was one of those spiral helicopter toys that you push up on a stick and it flies way up in the air. I played with this toy with my son Clayton in the front yard of Mommas house when he was about 11 years old in 2002. Aubree was not born until 2012.

How would she know about Clayton and I playing with this specific toy in the front yard? No one had ever talked about it or told her anything. She just popped up with it out of the blue. I believe she has a very special gift. Hopefully she will reveal much more to us as she gets older. She seems to have a large dose of what we always jokingly call "The family curse"

Chapter Eight
It Runs In The Family

I am and have always been very interested in my ancestry. Remembering my birth and everything that happened to me before and right after it probably has a lot to do with this. I also suppose I got some of this from my paternal grandmother. She always kept photo albums of all the family over the years and she shared them with me when we would visit her in Independence Missouri. I didn't get to visit regularly as we lived so far away, but when I did, she would show me her black and white photos contained in her numerous photo albums. She also kept boxes of photographs and would tell me who each person was and why they were important to her. Each person was important. Each person had a purpose for being there. No one was left out.

My grandmother's father Henry, my great grandfather, said his family came to America from Ireland. They sailed here on a big boat. He told of this incident to those of my family who were older than me such as my Daddy and my older brother Alan. Henry was born in June of 1865 in Missouri

My great grandfather was an Irishman, red hair, and all. He was born and lived in southern Missouri. He met the love of his life, my great grandmother Drushane at Fort Wiley in Kansas. The post was a base for skirmishes with Native Americans After the Civil War ended in 1865, during which time George A. Custer was stationed at the fort. My great grandmother Drushane was a Cherokee Indian and was also born in 1865. They were married at the tender age of 17. In the 1800's many men took Cherokee maidens to be their brides. Some people back then frowned on this. Some married out of necessity and some for love. My great grandparents did it for the latter. They raised 10 children, including my grandmother Christina. She was always proud of her Cherokee heritage. She instilled this pride in my father and me. Many back in those days looked down on Indians. My paternal grandfather, who married my grandmother Christina always told her to keep the fact she was Native American a secret. She was not to tell others in the community that she was half Cherokee. She, on the other hand, was very proud of her heritage. As my Daddy always was and as I am.

Sitting left **Great Grandpa Henry & Great Grandma Drushane on right. GG Grandma Martha (Henry's mother) in**

center. Grandma Christina standing on the left. Next to her is Cornelia and Cordelia. Sitting in front left side is Rosie and Celia. Picture taken around 1912.

There are many tales and stories that come from my grandmother and from my Daddy about our family. The Ozarks are steeped in mysterious tales and stories of folks who had powers beyond those of "normal" people. The family on the side of my paternal grandfather came here from the old Country. They came to America from England, Scotland, and Wales. Many of them were "warlocks" and "witches". This term back in the 1800's was a term given to those who had supernatural powers. Or in other words, they had unknown abilities to do things that weren't natural. It was not unusual back then to have a relative who could read tea leaves or who could draw a treasure map. Some of them could make a walking stick, chair, or a table dance around. All of these describe Daddy's great Uncle Bud. He had a twin sister which was my great grandmother Mary Addie.

Back in the days before television and internet, you visited with friends and family for your entertainment. You regularly had company in your home. This set the scene for Uncle Bud to show them his abilities, and all who witnessed these things, believed in them. Why not? When it boiled down to it, he had performed something no one else could do.

Back then, when you drank a cup of coffee, there would be grounds in the bottom of the cup. Uncle Bud would swish them around, look into the cup, and he could tell you your future. Daddy told me that one day they asked

Uncle Bud to draw a treasure map. Supposedly, there was Civil War gold buried in that part of the country. One neighbor apparently hit the jackpot after digging some up and moved to California with loads of money and was never to be seen or heard from ever again.

Uncle Bud did as they asked and drew a treasure map. He drew a sizeable oak tree. He said there was a large limb that came out from it and under that limb was a treasure. He gave them the area to search. All of them went out to find this tree in the dark of night. They were all so excited thinking they would be rich soon. They located the tree. All was as Uncle Bud had told them. But there in the dark of night was a foggy mist of a man sitting on the limb of that old oak tree. He seemed to be glowing like foxfire and a steamy mist was exuding from his form. Everyone was terrified and ran away. They returned during the daytime to try their luck again, but they saw the same misty figure of the old man on that limb a second time, still sitting there guarding his treasure that lie buried in the ground below…whatever it was. They never went back!

There was another time they asked Uncle Bud to draw a treasure map. He obliged them but he didn't understand what it was. Everyone followed the directions from his map. They found a cave. They began looking around. They had lanterns to light their way. They found a stash of silverware. Folks back then had Roger's silverware. There they found a counterfeit operation. Someone was melting the silverware to make silver coins. I don't know what ever became of this but once again, Uncle Bud's map was accurate! You always found something when he drew you a map. It was a well-known fact that you didn't argue with or question the warlocks or witches back then. You just took their word.

Great Uncle Bud with my great grandma, his twin sister Mary on the left and their sister Jennie on the right.

This side of my family is steeped in the history of warlocks. Great Uncle Bud's grandfather was also a warlock. This is my great, great, great grandfather. We have learned the hard way to never utter his name. You don't dare say his name or hang his photograph in your house. My daughter Amber and I have both experienced the consequences of doing so.

I, being the type of person who is very interested in family history, found a photo of my great, great, great grandfather in a book of McAnally descendants. I had a copy of the photo made as well as one of his wife, my great, great, great grandmother Jane. I framed and hung the photos of both of them in my house. Hers still hangs there to this day.

My great, great, great Grandmother Jane Warren East.

I had his picture hanging right beside a grandfather clock. Every time I would walk into the room, the clock's glass door would be open. I would shut it. Then after a while, it would open again. I would shut it once again. We also occasionally caught a glimpse of a black shadow passing by this clock. One day his photo in the frame was crooked. I took it down to adjust it. When I opened the back of it, the glass shattered, and it cut my hand. It was a deep slice. I decided that maybe he was unhappy about me having his picture hanging up. After all, the clock door continuously opened. And the black shadow. Then his photo somehow became crooked in the frame and when I tried to fix it, the glass mysteriously shattered and cut me. I put his photo away, back into the family history book. The clock door never opened again. We also never saw the black shadowy figure walking by the clock anymore after that. I learned he did not want his photo to be shown. I told him I would not ever hang it up again. All the trouble stopped. Until….

I was talking to my daughter about how he did not have a headstone at his grave. There was only a rock there with his initials engraved on it. I found this while doing a search on my Ancestry.com page for any information I could find out about him. After my daughter and I talked, things started happening again.

I had a shirt hanging in the doorway between my kitchen and living room to dry. It started flailing around wildly. There was no breeze inside. No windows or doors were open. There were no fans on, and I do not have central heat or air. It simply started swinging around. Then a pen flew out of a partially opened drawer in the kitchen. I immediately yelled out "I will find your grave! I will get you a headstone! Please just stop!" And all the activity stopped. At least at my house. My daughters house, well, that's another story…

Years later, my daughter Amber and I were talking about this. We were using his name as we talked about what happened. My daughter was then an adult and lived in her own house. She went to the basement to a walk-in closet to get her shoes. As she stood in this closet, a large fluorescent light bulb that was leaning up in the corner, suddenly just exploded into a million pieces. She had not touched it or anything else in the closet. She was not anywhere near it. Again, with the glass. There's something about glass…

There was another time Amber was telling a friend of hers about how we had warlocks in the family. They went to look at this photo of him online and mentioned his name as well. Later the same day, Amber was in her kitchen. She had purchased a set of 4 glasses that were her favorite ones. One was sitting on the drying mat beside the sink. She was on the other side of the room as she watched this glass fly off of the countertop. It flew through the air all the way across the room and dropped onto the ground and shattered. How did this happen? Again, with the glass. There's something about glass…

I did a little research online about the connection between glass and witchcraft. What I found was Olde English witch balls. This is what I found on the Wikipedia website. "A witch ball is a hollow sphere of glass. Historically, witch balls were hung in cottage windows in the 17th and 18th century England (where he came from) to ward off evil spirits, witches, evil spells, ill fortune, and bad spirits. The witch's ball is still today used extensively throughout Sussex, England and continues to hold great superstition with regard to warding off evil spirits. The tradition was also taken to overseas British colonies and remains popular in coastal regions."

So, the glass is supposed to trap any negative spirits and keep them at bay. Is he telling us that glass does not affect his ability to do whatever he chooses to do? That it holds no power over him. Your guess is as good as mine.

I am now questioning my decision to write anything about this. I hesitate as I continue. As I was doing a bit of research while writing this particular section of this book, I began once again to see the black shadow walking through the living room. I've seen it about 4 times today. I was also on the phone today with Amber, trying to get the details correct about her experience with the light bulb and the glass breaking. As I talked to her, being extremely careful not to mention his name or talk in too much detail, a cold blast of air hit me. Simultaneously, I heard three loud raps originating from somewhere inside the house. I hesitate now to add this portion to the book. If it was not so important to the information I am recording about my family, I would exclude it. But as it is, these facts need to be recorded for future generations. They need to know these things so as to not make the same mistake I did.

Daddy told me about another friend of theirs who would visit their home when he was a child. This man was also a warlock. He always carried a walking stick with him. He did not need it to walk but would go nowhere without it in his hand. Not even walking from one room to another. He could make his walking stick get up and dance around. There were no strings. He could also sit in one room and look into another room such as the kitchen. He would make the chairs move around all by themselves. No one knew how this happened and again, you didn't question a warlock. It was against every code of conduct back then.

I not only got the "witchery" in my blood on the McAnally side, I got some from my Mommas side as well. My momma told of her father's family visiting them when she was a child. Uncles in particular. They would not let the children watch but somehow Momma knew about how they made a table get up and float around the room.

My Nanny, Momma's momma, had the ability to heal you if you got a bad burn. It would not even leave a scar. This ability was passed from a male of the family to a female of the next generation. Then from the female to a male of the next generation. Unfortunately, Nanny only had girls and didn't pass it on.

One time my cousin got scalding hot water spilled all over her. She was sure to have third degree burns. But as soon as it happened, Nanny started working on her. Momma said Nanny would lick her finger and start rubbing a circle around the burn or burns, mumbling something under her breath. She just kept doing this. We don't know what she was saying unfortunately because she failed to pass it down to anyone. I'm not sure how long it took or how she knew when to stop, but it worked. My cousin, who should have had terrible scars and burns all over her face and body, did not have one blemish on her skin. She was completely healed without any scars. How is that possible?

There were many superstitions and old wives tales back then. Never walk under a ladder. If a black cat ran in front of you, you turned around and went back home and you started over. These are just some of the things that people back then believed in. They would never take any chances with any of these things. This was serious business, and you didn't question it. You just did what you were told you should do in any type of circumstance you found yourself in to avoid any type of calamity befalling you. Looking back at this, I'm sure there were reasons they believed in the way that they did. Something must have happened at some point and time to convince them that it was not a good idea to ignore these things and if they did, there would be consequences.

Maybe we should not be in such a hurry to disregard these things either. It made sense to them back then. Old ways are usually the best.

Chapter nine
Visitations

I will confess, losing Daddy was the hardest, most unbearable grief I had ever been through. I would go to him with all my troubles, and he would always have an answer. He was my best friend, and I could talk to him about anything. Regretfully, he passed away in November of 2003. To get this story going in the right direction, I'll tell you of a conversation we had long before his passing. This conversation will be relevant as the chapter progresses.

We used to sit and talk a lot. Often, I'd visit with him all day long. He was so much older than me, it was like having a dad and a grandpa all rolled into one. We talked about so many different things. One of our favorite subjects was the Bible. Then there was the discussion about what it will be like to die. We agreed that whichever one of us passed away first would come back in some fashion to let the other one know what it was like.

Unfortunately, the time came for him to go. Unbearable heartache overwhelmed me. My birthday was approaching about 3 weeks after he passed and needless to say, it was not a joyful birthday for me. I was so brokenhearted, wishing we could have one of our talks again. I went into his room and sat down. Looking at all of the photos hanging on the wall sent overwhelming sadness over me.

Because I have always heard spirits and voices from beyond and at times captured them on a recorder, I decided to take out my phone and turn on the audio recorder, just hoping I might hear his voice. I sat there silently with the recorder running. Later, I played the recording to see if there was anything on it. To my surprise, I heard his voice! He said "Hey! Hey! Hey Dawn…look at me!" I was so happy to hear his voice again! Then he said, "Happy birthday." How wonderful to hear his voice again. That year I got what I wanted for my birthday after all. He came to see me and talk with me in the only way he could under the circumstances. I only wish I had known he was there at the time that I was recording. In another visitation later on, he told me that he knew and was happy that I heard his salutation and birthday greeting for me on that day.

He has come to me more than once in my "dreams". I hesitate to call them dreams here because they are not really dreams. They are visitations. He visits me at times when I am asleep.

One such occasion happened 3 months after he had passed, I had a horrible dream. I was being chased by some terrible people on the street. They were shooting at me. I gasped as I was struck in the chest with a bullet. Everything started fading away as I fell onto the street beside the curb. My worst fear had come true. I was crying frantically. It got darker and darker, and I knew I was dying.

Suddenly, I saw a very bright, shimmering light. So bright, in fact, that it was blinding. This light radiated from the end of a very long tunnel. I saw a figure start to appear there in the center of the light. This figure was completely engulfed in this golden light, and the figure also seemed to emanate its own light as well. As it approached me, I started to make out features. It was Daddy!

His visage was absolutely glowing. He was so young. Flawless skin and his hair perfectly combed like he always wanted it to be. His eyes sparkled big and blue unlike when he was alive and had cataracts. He was very young. When I was born, he was 45 years old. I never saw him when he was young except in photographs. But there he stood before me, absolutely gleaming and youthful. Words cannot express what I saw. His appearance was perfect, unlike the flaws that we all have here.

I only saw him from the waist up. The light was so bright that it concealed the rest of his body. He was wearing some type of long, white shirt or robe. On it, appeared to be three name tags. Two on the left and one on the right, though I could not read what they said.

Though he did not speak to me, his smile and countenance seemed to convey the message of total happiness and peacefulness. I had never imagined him in this way in my wildest dreams. Then I remembered the last thing he told me before he passed away. He said, "Pretty soon, I'm going to be your age and you're going to be my age." About 9 hours later he passed. At that time, his words didn't make a lot of sense to me. But they do now. He is young again. He is not old anymore.

I told Momma about the dream, and she said that maybe the name tags were for me, my sister and her. Maybe he was telling me that he still carries us with him. I do know that he kept his promise to me. During that horrible dream of being shot and dying, he came back to show me what it is like when you die. Just like we promised we would do whenever one of us passed away. Thank you, Daddy, for keeping your promise!

Those are not the only times he has visited me. One day, while I was home, I stood in my living room sadly looking at a photo of him that was framed and sitting on top of my television. As I turned to go into the other room, that picture came flying off of the tv. It landed halfway across the room and even broke the frame. I was not even close to the picture as I stood looking at it before turning to walk away. At first, I was shocked. Then I just laughed and said, "Good one Daddy!"

There was another time a little later that I had another "dream". I still remember the details vividly. After I woke, I wrote down everything that he had told me as we talked during this visitation. This time he looked like his usual self. Not the young man he was in the other visitation. I felt more at ease speaking with him as he appeared the way I remember him in his later years. I suppose that must be the reason he appeared to me in that way.

We talked about all sorts of things that night. Looking back, I wish I had asked him about more things before he had to leave again. I mentioned to him that I heard his voice on my audio recorder saying Happy Birthday. He said "Yes! I was standing right beside you!" I explained to him that I didn't hear him at the time until I listened to the recording when I arrived home. He was happy that I had heard him and he told me that he was trying very hard to let me know that he was there for my birthday.

I asked him about the haunted house that we as a family have occupied for so long and still do to this day. About the old man in overalls who would visit his room and try to wake him telling him to "Get up!". He replied, "It was Henry. I found out who that was too soon" leading me to believe he did not like this man. The man who originally built the house in the 1800's was named Henry. The founder of the town we lived in.

He told me about another man he saw there in the old house. He said his name was Mann. Remember that name because it will become very important later on in the next chapter. I am guessing at the spelling because he only told me his name. I assumed if it was a name, it would not be spelled Man.

He also told me about a judge as well and explained that this judge was pacing the floor. He showed me that this judge was occupying the area of my childhood bedroom.

He spoke of another man there whose name was Everette. He said that Everette was "a pain to be around." That he was a very grumpy man. This man had "control of the switch." He explained to me that the switch is a place for people who have passed over to go so they can visit and check on loved ones who remain here. Everette didn't like anyone visiting the switch.

I also asked him about a friend of ours who had passed away from cancer. Her name was Diane and her and Daddy were close friends. He said "Yes, Diane's relatives were going wild right before she got here. They were stomping their feet when she pulled up." He also said she had been too quick to go to the switch trying to visit her family that were still alive. I guess one is supposed to wait awhile before doing so. But he only waited about 3 weeks before visiting me on my birthday.

He then told me he had visited me at home a couple of times since he had passed. He told me there was something seriously wrong with my house that needed immediate attention. Not long after that, I found out I had a termite problem and had to replace most of my kitchen floor and a large portion of one wall. He had warned me.

Then I asked him if he had gotten his mansion yet as it says we will in the bible. "In my Father's house are many mansions. If it were not so, I would have told you. I go to prepare a place for you" as Jesus told us in John 14:2. Daddy said "Not yet. I haven't got to pick my house yet" inferring to me that when we die, our mansion is there, but we won't reside in it until the end when Jesus returns to bring all of His children home to be in Heaven with Him.

You may think this is a lot of nonsense and my imagination or actually a dream instead of a visitation. I beg to differ with you. If you do believe it's my imagination, keep on reading. I will show you proof that this particular visitation revealed more to me than I thought at the time. "Mr. Mann" is real. I could not have made something like that up or just dreamed it out of the blue.

Do you recall that I told you to remember the man Daddy said was named Mann? Let's continue…

Chapter 10

Mr. "Mann"

As I mentioned to you in the last chapter, Daddy had told me that there was a spirit of a man named Mann there in the old house on Spruce Street. That did not make much sense to me, as I had never heard of anyone having that name. I thought maybe I had heard wrong or misunderstood. Not so. I would find out later that it was not a misunderstanding.

One day, 13 years later, my daughter Amber and I went to the local library to do a little research to see if we could find out anything that may have happened in the past or any information about the house at all. We ran onto a newspaper article on microfilm dated February 19, 1916. It seems there was a house a block and a half from the downtown square that had caught on fire. It was the grandest house that was there in 1869 and was even used as a hotel for a time. It was the first frame building in the town. The other homes in the area at that time were log cabins. It was erected by the same man who built our house and owned the property our house was built on. The same man who founded our town.

It seems this house was rented by a family. The man's last name was MANUS. While they were away, waiting on a train, the house caught fire and burned down. I will tell you now to remember the fact that they were waiting on a train when it burned down. This will be important later on.

The newspaper article said not much was saved. This house was only 3 blocks from where our house was built a few years later and owned by the same man who built both houses. Oddly, we found charred boards that had been in a fire in the house we lived in. There were additions to the original house that were added in later years. The wood that was salvaged from the house that burned down was used in the construction of the additions to our house.

Now, let's revisit the fact that 13 years prior to finding this old newspaper article in the library, Daddy had come to me in a "dream" and told me there was the spirit of a man in our house and his name was Mann. And, also remember the fact that the wood salvaged from his house that burned was used in the construction of additions to our house. Is it a coincidence that the man whose house burned had the last name of Manus? I don't think so. I believe this is the one Daddy was referring to as Mann thirteen years earlier. But wait, there is more…

As you have already learned from reading previous chapters, I use my audio recorder regularly to try to piece the puzzle together of what is going on in that house. One day in 2004, I was standing in Daddy's bedroom in front of a roaring fire that was in the wood stove. I decided to turn the recorder on my phone on to see if I could capture anything at all. I let it play for a couple of minutes as I stood there completely still with no noises that I could hear with my own ears. This was long before we had found the newspaper article or did any type of research at the library.

When I replayed the recording, I couldn't believe what I heard. There was a man mumbling and going on about something the entire length of the recording. But I couldn't make out the words. All the while, I could hear what sounded like a train rolling along. You could hear the metal whistling as it rolled down the tracks. It went on and on. Then suddenly there was a loud "BEEP, BEEP, BEEP, BEEP!" The same sound you hear when a large truck is backing up to warn you it is moving. Then I heard the man exclaim "It's here!! It's here!!" and he began cackling wildly just like the Big Black Mean Man. Then the recording ended. It had the same voice that the black, ominous figure had that chased me out of my bedroom so many years ago.

40th YEAR Feb 19, 1916 ████████

AN OLD LANDMARK OF ████████ GONE.

BIG FIRE WEDNESDAY MORNING DESTROYS THE OLDEST BUILDING IN ALL THIS SECTION.

Shortly after six o'clock Wednesday morning fire completely destroyed the ████████ residence, a block and a half west of the public square. It was occupied by ███ Manus who, with his family was up early to catch the six o'clock train, and it was thought that the fire originated in the room where they had prepared breakfast. Everything in the room was in flames when the fire was discovered and the first parties arrived from the ████ Hotel across the street. Very little of the furnishings were saved, and, although the fire company did good work, the building was a complete loss, the walls on the south left standing being of no value whatever. $1,500 insurance was carried on the building.

Although there were several log houses standing in town when Capt. ████████ began the erection of this residence in 1869, this was the first frame building in Harrison, and was the oldest house in town. It might be said that the city from its earliest day has been built about this structure.

In the earlier days it was used as a hotel, when it was considered the largest and best in all North Arkansas.

Since coming into the hands of Mr. ████ the grounds especially have been much improved and it was considered one of the beauty spots of the town. Only last fall he purchased a more desirable residence in the north part of town, and since that time it has been rented.

It is likely that the grounds will be cut up into smaller lots for residence purposes.

Previous page: newspaper article from 1916 showing the house that burned with a man in a horse and buggy out front. Names and locations blacked out for privacy. Notice the last name of Manus underlined in red by me.

> Shortly after six o'clock Wednesday morning fire completely destroyed the ▓▓▓▓▓▓▓ residence, a block and a half west of the public square. It was occupied by ▓▓ Manus who, with his family was up early to catch the six o'clock train, and it was thought that the fire originated in the room where they had prepared breakfast. Everything in the room was in flames when the fire was discovered and the first parties arrived from the ▓▓▓▓ Hotel across the street. Very little of the furnishings were saved, and, although the fire

Now another thing. Notice the photo in this newspaper article. You see the house and a horse and buggy sitting in front of it with a fellow sitting in the buggy. Notice what the man is wearing. A black derby hat and a big black coat.

Close up cropped and zoomed in on the man in the buggy. See his black derby hat and black coat.

I'm convinced the man in this photograph is the "Big Black Mean Man". His spirit followed the wood salvaged from his house that burned down to our house when it was used for an addition to our house. This is the "Mann" Daddy told me about 13 years earlier in my "dream". This was the man who while waiting for a train, had his

78

home burn to the ground. I heard the train. I heard him exclaiming "It's here! It's here!" Like I said, there are no coincidences. Just a mysterious puzzle that seems to be coming together.

Mr. Manus's train has finally arrived…and so the strangeness continues.

I need to write one last thing here. Just last night as I was on the phone with Amber, she sent me a screenshot of someone who sent her a friend request on Facebook. A random guy whom she had no mutual friends with or was not in any mutual groups with. In disbelief and shock, I saw his name on the screenshot. His name was Ed Mann!

Is Mr. Manus upset about me writing this chapter about him? I guess we will never know for sure, but it certainly is a coincidence she got that friend request the same day I wrote this chapter…or is it?

Chapter 11

The Face of Jesus

As I stated in an earlier chapter, I have pre-birth memories. I was in a glorious place, walking hand in hand with a "man". I was a child, and He was an adult. The place where we walked had rainbow skies and treetops that glistened in the light. I vividly remember this. This man talked with me without moving His mouth. I could "hear" Him speaking to me. His face is etched into my memory, and I remember every detail of His appearance.

Not long ago, I saw a tv show about the Shroud of Turin. It was called "The Real Face of Jesus?" having a question mark at the end of the title questioning whether it really was His face or not.

The centuries old shroud contains a faint impression of the front and back of a human body along with blood, dirt, and water stains from its age. This man was tortured, beaten and had all the brutal markings Jesus would have had on His body from what we read about in the Bible about His crucifixion. Computer artist Ray Downing of Studio Macbeth in New York City, who specializes in digital illustration and animation was very dedicated to work long and hard on this. The project took a year to complete. They used a team of graphic artists and the newest available technology to create a computer-generated image. They went to extensive lengths recreating the face that was on the shroud. Ultimately, we got to see the completed image of the face on the shroud.

I could not believe what I saw. Tears immediately filled my eyes. This face was the same one etched into my memory. The "man" on the shroud was the same one I had seen before. It was Jesus. His eyes, the prominent brow, the shape of His nose…everything was exactly as I had seen Him before. The only difference was the color of His eyes. His eyes were brown in the recreation. Jesus's eyes are sparkling blue. Of course, they would not have known this detail from the Shroud.

I know this is contradictory to the fact that most people in Judea and Egypt around that time had brown eyes and olive colored skin. But He does not have brown eyes. I clearly saw His eyes myself as I looked at Him and walked and talked with Him.

Is this because He was sent from Heaven by the Father and maybe His genetics were a bit different than the Jews of the day? Of course, I am speculating on this matter. Possibly, He did have brown eyes during the 33 years He resided here on earth. Nevertheless, He did not when I was with Him. I do not know about that, but I do know His eyes are not brown now.

I often go look at the pictures and paintings they have recreated from the shroud. Just to see a visible, tangible image of that beautiful, loving face that I saw before. I cry sometimes just longing to be with Him again. I miss being there with Him as I was before. I know some day I will return to Him.

"Then shall the dust return to the earth as it was: and the spirit shall return unto God who gave it." Ecclesiastes 12:7

I know for a FACT that the man on the Shroud of Turin is my Lord. And now you do as well!

Chapter 12

Evil Antiquities

Now we will take a drastic 360-degree turn. Just as there are heavenly beings of light and love, there are also spiritual forces of darkness at work. Ephesian 6:12 reads "For we wrestle not against flesh and blood, but against principalities, against powers, against the rulers of the darkness of this world, against spiritual wickedness in high places."

Where do I begin? Numerous times, I have purchased items and lamented doing so later. Paranormal oddities and strangeness seem to follow me everywhere I go. These are accounts of some of the things I, unknowingly at the time, brought home with me. The point here being…be careful what you buy. Especially if it is an antique or old collectible. You may get more than what you bargained for.

Once such occurrence happened when I was at a children's ministry thrift store. I spotted a spectacular antique picture of The Last Supper in a golden, metal frame. It also had a light on it so the picture could be illuminated. It was gorgeous and it was only 5 dollars. I grabbed it up and was so delighted about what I had found. It wasn't long before I suspected that it had come with a little something extra.

I took the picture home but didn't hang it up right away. I wanted to find the perfect spot for it with an outlet nearby so I could plug it in and illuminate it. Soon after I took it home, I started hearing a lot of random banging noises around the house. At times, I would hear a very distinct "knock, knock, knock!" on what sounded like the side of the house. I would go outside and walk the entire perimeter of the house. There was never anything or anyone found.

Another time I heard what sounded like someone had dropped a heavy wooden pallet on the roof. I was positive someone was trying to break into the house. I grabbed the only weapon I could find at the time, a machete, and made my way into each and every room in the house. I found nothing. I patrolled the entire perimeter of the house, even checking on the roof for prowlers or animals…I found nothing.

As well as hearing clamorous noises around the house, out of the corner of my eye, I began seeing small black shadows crawling around the house. I likened it to a giant tarantula. I saw these many times.

Then, I hung the picture…

I eventually found the perfect spot to hang the picture. It was beautiful to see it lit up. I was so pleased with it. I worked all afternoon cleaning and straightening up the room that it was in. That night when I went to sleep, I woke several times to see something tall and black floating beside my bed. It appeared to be a black, hooded, cloaked figure. Each time, when it realized that I saw it, it would instantaneously speed away, passing through the wall. Needless to say, I didn't sleep very well that night.

When I woke up the next morning, I had a horrible feeling of dread and foreboding. I was riddled with anxiety, and I didn't know why. In order to get to the kitchen, I had to walk through the room where the picture was hanging. An instant feeling of terror rushed over me. A very heavy sensation. The air was as thick as butter. It felt like there were a hundred sets of eyes watching me and surrounding me. It felt like pure evil, and I didn't understand what was happening to me. I just knew that I could not go back into the room where the illuminated picture was hanging.

In sheer panic, I called my daughter Amber for help. As she drove to my house, an unexpected, out of the blue, flash flood was making it almost impossible for her to get there. It was raining so hard she could barely see the road. Was this entity trying to keep her away?

She finally arrived at my house. I explained to her what was happening. In terror, we entered the room, unplugged the light, and took the picture off the wall. We placed it in a plastic bag. I laid it on the floor of the living room and walked into the kitchen. As Amber sat in the living room, she saw a large black figure float out of the room it had previously been hanging in and hovered in the next room. As I turned to come back into the living room, she said it vanished into thin air as I moved toward it. She didn't tell me about seeing it until later because she didn't want to frighten me further, as if that was even possible.

I think whatever was attached to that picture was energized with power when I plugged it in, lit it up, and put it on display. Having done that, the house became filled with what I can only describe as an evil energy. It was horrific.

We drove in the flash flood to dispose of it. I was desperate to rid myself of this thing. We could scarcely see the road. I abandoned it outside at the thrift store because the store was closed. I left it sitting there by the dock doors in the pouring rain and we sped away as fast as we could. Hopefully the rain destroyed it, and they threw the dreadful thing in the garbage.

Funny thing about it, the downpour and storm stopped after I left the picture sitting there on the concrete, alone and deserted. All I can say is good riddance.

There was another time that I was shopping for end tables and a coffee table for the new living room we had built on to the house. I wanted good quality tables made with solid wood. I found a set of two end tables and a coffee table at a flea market. They were solid birch wood and were beautiful. I jumped on the chance to get them at only $125. We brought them home and they were perfect. Or at least, in my initial assessment, they were.

As the days passed, many times as I sat at the kitchen table, I would see a black shadow passing from one side of the living room to the other. I was always home alone, and it was quite eerie. This happened multiple times and I eventually told my husband Eric about what I was experiencing. I knew that the only thing we had brought into the house recently were those tables and I suspected they may be to blame.

We decided to do a little investigating. One night when he was home, I got out my phone and turned on the audio recorder. My "go to" for any odd activity I am experiencing. So as the recorder was running Eric said, "Are these tables special to you or what?" To our surprise, when we replayed the recording, we heard an answer…"YES!" It was a loud despairing female voice, and she sounded very disturbed and desperate. I immediately told him "Get these tables out of this house!" so he carried them outside and put them in the camper.

But as time went on and days later, I was still seeing the black shadow pacing back and forth in the living room. I could handle no more of this. I asked my son Clayton to help me load the tables up in my car. Clayton, Momma, and I drove back to the flea market where I had purchased them. I asked the man there who had sold them to me if I could return them. He asked me why I didn't want them. I felt like an idiot, but I explained to him what had happened. That they were haunted and whoever owned them prior to me was extremely upset about it. He didn't believe me. He looked at me like I was from another planet. Momma jumped in and said, "She has a recording of the spirit answering their question. Do you want to hear it?" He immediately started shaking his head and swinging his hands in the air saying "NO, NO, NO! And I don't want those tables back in my store either!" We had to leave the store with the tables still in our possession. I desperately wanted to dispose of them.

There was a used furniture store in town, so I drove there hoping to at least get a portion of my money back. To my relief the man at the store wanted to purchase them from me. He gave me sixty dollars. So, I made back almost half of what I paid. I didn't care if I lost money on the deal. I just wanted to rid myself of them and whatever was attached to them.

The next day, I drove past that store. The tables were sitting outside in the front of the store in the parking lot. They sat there for a couple of weeks and then were finally gone. Had the spirit haunting them frightened the store owner as well?

Hopefully whoever purchased them is not sensitive to the spirit world. Some people are oblivious to it, and it doesn't bother them. My Momma being one of them when I was younger.

I later found 2 end tables and a coffee table at two different yard sales. I questioned each of the individuals about the origin of the tables and made sure I could purchase them without bringing home more problems. I asked the sellers about the owners of the tables prior to me, and if that person was still alive. I felt really foolish, but I wanted no more haunted objects and unhappy spirits in my house. They asked why I was asking and thought it was strange until I explained to them why I was inquiring. Then, they understood. Or at least they told me that they did and said they didn't blame me for being cautious after all I had been through.

How do I always manage to get stuck with haunted objects? These are not the only times this has happened to me. I have another one to tell you about.

As I told you in an earlier chapter, I am an old soul. I love all things antique. I think I entered this world in the wrong century. Anyway, as a child, my grandma Christina would give me things like salt and pepper shakers, doilies, kitchen wear etc. and tell me that when I was old enough, I could use them in my own home. I especially loved the salt and pepper shakers. She gave me ducks and squirrels and I thought the animals were so cute. So, I have always enjoyed collecting vintage shakers. I have about 100 sets now and have even started a collection to give to my granddaughter Aubree when she is older.

There was a certain shaker set that I had always wanted. It was a set of white Christmas angels with spaghetti trim on them. They were beautiful and very hard to find and were also very expensive. I found a set on eBay for a steal. They were only twenty-five dollars. These normally sold for around one hundred and twenty dollars. I snatched them up and was so excited for my good fortune. Or so I thought.

They arrived and it was around Christmas, so I displayed them on the fireplace beside the tree and other Christmas decorations. As time passed, I began to hear a crinkling noise in my ear each night as I sat watching television. It sounded like cellophane rattling and being crinkled together. I was curious as to what was causing this. And by this time, I was suspicious when I purchased anything used or old. I once again got out the audio recorder on the phone. I sat silently one day as I was there alone in the room with the shakers. When I listened back to the recording, I was shocked. I heard a gruff, angry voice of a man. It sounded a bit like Mr. Manus's voice had on the other recordings, so I wasn't sure if it was him or someone else who came along with the newest addition to the room.

I did not want to get rid of my prized shakers. I had what I thought was a brilliant idea. I asked my daughter Amber to take them home with her for a few days to see if anything strange happened to her. I did not reveal to her what I was experiencing with the weird crinkling cellophane noise in my ear. She agreed and took them home for a test. She began to hear the crinkling noise right beside her ear and she told me about her experience. Our stories corroborated and to my dismay, the shakers were the culprit. I couldn't keep them. I sadly sold them again on eBay for the same amount I paid for them. I just wanted to dispose of them. And not everyone is sensitive to these things.

I have to add this as an afterthought. This **just** happened. I was on the phone with Amber last night. Four days ago, there was an out of the blue, random storm that delivered three inches of rain in less than an hour. Amber got washed across the road in her car as she was trying to return home. Her car died and she had to call a tow truck.

Her motor was full of water. Other smaller cars went through the water with no problem.

This happened on the same day that I wrote this chapter about the sudden, out of the blue storm she had to drive through to get to my house that had happened years ago. When she came over to help me get rid of that religious picture. Coincidence? I don't think so.

Chapter 13
Realizing The Impossible

You would think by now that I would be accustomed to odd and unusual things happening and not even bat an eye anymore. After all, I have seen it all, right? Not so my friend. There is always more. So much more!

One night, me, my late husband and a friend of ours were driving on a dark, deserted, gravel road heading home from a trip to the river. We made a wrong turn, and we were completely disoriented. We were many miles out in the middle of the woods, and we couldn't seem to find our way home no matter which way we turned. We drove for hours.

As we rounded a corner deep in the woods, there in the trees, silently floating, was a craft of some sort. A golden sphere with flashing-colored lights emanating from multiple fixtures that surrounded it on all sides. It measured approximately 3 to 4 feet around. I say it was floating because it made absolutely no noise. There it was, gliding silently approximately 20 feet off of the ground, maneuvering its way around each and every tree. It flashed different colors from each light fixture intermittently all around this "ball", but always kept a steady white light on the ground below it as if it was scanning the ground. It was so bright, so illuminated, that you could see everything within 50 feet of this object easily. The woods surrounding it were glowing brightly.

And we were in the dead of night in the middle of the dark woods with nothing and no one anywhere near us. There was not a soul out there but the three of us…and this thing, whatever it was.

Each of us in the car saw it. We started panicking. Our friend screamed "GO! GO! GO!". I was driving and I took off like a shot. I was on an unfamiliar dirt road with many twists and turns. I drove as fast as I could to escape a certain doom and put as much distance between us and this thing as I could. I do not know how I managed to keep the car out of the ditches. Finally, around 4 am, we found a house and saw someone standing outside. We asked for directions out of there. That was an extremely long and terrifying night.

But that was not the only time I saw what I will come right out and call a UFO. Get it over with and just say it. I saw a UFO. Remember what I said earlier. If it looks like a duck, quacks like a duck….

Another time me and a friend were returning to her house late at night, and we took the shortcut to her house which was on a lonely gravel road. Nothing unusual was happening when suddenly we saw something in the sky. There were 3 lights. They were in a triangular pattern. I do not remember the color of the lights. It seems they were white and blue, but I would not swear to that. It must be an airplane we rationalized and told each other. But then we realized this "airplane" was not moving. It was not making any noise whatsoever. It was simply floating above her car. We stopped the car, and I hung my head out the window. Looking back, I think that is the dumbest thing I could have ever done.

It hovered there above the car and maneuvered its way so that it was directly above us. We watched it for about 2 minutes just levitating there. Then in an instant, it zipped away and vanished behind the dark silhouette of the mountains to our right. It moved with such speed, you could scarcely blink that quickly. It was instantaneous. It flew with great force and simply vanished. But never made a noise.

We looked at each other in shock. She told me, "Please don't tell anyone what we just saw. They will think we are crazy!" But when we returned to her house where other friends were waiting, we eventually "spilled the beans" and they all got a good laugh out of it. But some believed us. It happened and we both knew it. There was no denying it.

Speaking of UFO's, I have to mention a story Momma shared with me about something that happened to her when she was a child. If you know my Momma at all, you know she will not admit to anything that is wild or unusual that happens to her. She keeps everything like that a secret and rarely shares it with anyone. But as she has realized through the years that so many odd things happen to me and I freely share them with her and others, it's ok to share some of these things. That people won't judge her or label her as crazy. And if they do, who really cares?

She told me of something that she experienced as a child. There was a creek behind their home and a field there as well. One day, while she was at the creek, she glanced up and spotted what she described as a silver metal disk. She said it looked like a pie pan with a round dome on the top and that it just floated there in the air above the trees. This was in the 1940's. There was no such aircraft back then that looked like this or moved like this. It moved slowly across the sky until it vanished. She says she can remember it clearly to this day, vividly in her mind.

What are these crafts we are seeing. Does seeing these crafts, these UFO's, run in the family? My daughter has also seen them. Are we all crazy? Is it a coincidence? Like I said, I don't believe in coincidences.

Chapter 14
Bigfoot - The Introduction

Where do I begin? I have been "doing this" for approximately 9 years now. I was always interested in bigfoot, even as a child. Back in the 1970's, it was a big attraction with carnivals traveling around that supposedly had a monster bigfoot inside a cage. You could go inside and see it for a price. Daddy took me inside one of these on one occasion and it scared the pants off of me! But he was just as curious as I was and wanted to see what was growling so loudly in there. Even though it was only a guy in a costume rattling the cage bars and roaring wildly, to me, it was possible because after all, I had seen the "impossible" my entire life.

I have always been drawn to the paranormal. Anything that seems to be "out of the norm", simply because of what I have experienced during my entire lifetime. And it seems to be drawn to me as well. I love watching television shows about ghosts, ufo's and anything unusual. Eventually, the subject of Bigfoot reared its head again when I watched a few documentaries about it. Once again, my curiosity was peaked. I noticed that some of the things that these people were seeing and contributing to bigfoot activity were things that I was also finding.

Tree structures that were intricately made. Woven over and under and that could not have naturally fallen that way. Large rock stacks made with rocks that are humanly impossible to lift. "Animal" noises that I had heard but could not explain. The "bionic bird call" being one of them.

Oa side note, I later found out what this was called and that this had been heard by others. It literally sounds like a bird that is the size of a brahma bull. And then silence. No movement. No flying. Nothing. I stood there for around 15 to 20 minutes looking all around and saw nor heard a thing afterwards. And the sound was so close to me, you would think I'd have seen or heard something.

At times I'd also hear tree knocks. Find odd stick formations on the ground. And the list goes on. I was intrigued and began looking at my surroundings armed with the new knowledge I had obtained. I went out in the woods to do a little more scouting around. I looked at things I was seeing with a skeptic's perspective. How did this happen? Is it possible that a human could have done this? I was determined to find out the truth.

On one particular day, my husband and I, along with my daughter Amber and her husband DJ and three of our grandchildren went hiking in the woods we frequently visited.

As we were hiking along, I was teasing the children about how we may see bigfoot. You know, as a child, you have a very vivid imagination and things like this tend to stick with you. Later in life, you hold them as cherished memories. I wanted the kids to have that memory of me and them going on an adventure together when they grew up. I taught them how investigators call for bigfoot and how they would hit trees with sticks to attract their attention and sometimes even receive a knock back. Yes, I know, I was still in the stone age, but this is how it all began.

The kids playfully whooped as I had taught them and called for fun as we hiked our way along the narrow trail. As we got further along, deeper into the woods, a deer suddenly popped out of a nearby brush pile that it had been hiding in and ran directly towards us. It passed by us so closely, that we could have reached out and touched it. This deer was obviously frightened and was running away from something that was much more threatening to it than we were.

We also noticed there was a pile of deer leg bones where we were standing. The rest of the carcasses were gone. I have heard a theory that Bigfoot will break the legs off of their prey when hunting so they cannot run away. It sounds like this theory may be correct. That seemed to be the case here because that is what we all saw.

As we walked a bit further, we were all standing on a low water bridge. As we stood there, we heard an ear splitting, ungodly noise. It started out as a low pitch "WHOOOOOOO!" noise. Then it started building momentum. Gradually, getting louder and louder and reaching a deafening higher pitch. It then progressed to what I can only describe as simulating a tornado siren. As loud as it would be if you were standing right beside it.

But we were in the middle of the woods. This made absolutely no sense.

The thunderous noise continued on in one long, continuous deafening howl for what seemed like an eternity until it winded down to an inhuman, vocal, guttural growl. That resounding noise was so loud that you could **feel** it and it was not far away.

Amber and I stood there staring at each other in disbelief at what we had just witnessed. Whatever made this noise had to have the lung capacity of at least an elephant to do this. No wonder the deer came running towards us. It was trying to escape a certain doom. And we, unknowingly, had interrupted the bigfoots hunt and it sounded as though he was pretty upset about the whole thing.

This was the first encounter we all had together and the first encounter that showed my daughter and her husband that bigfoot is real. I was not crazy! Bigfoot IS real!

This was my eye-opening introduction to the reality that I was, in fact, seeing evidence of bigfoot activity all around me. They were here and they were living right under our noses this entire time. "How could I have been so blind for all of these years?" I thought to myself.

I was then obsessed with documenting the things I was finding at this point. I consistently carried my phone so that I would have a camera with me at all times. I began taking photos of all I was discovering, and documenting it. I also began taking videos so I could explain what I was seeing. This started a whole new era for me.

Chapter 15
Gathering Evidence – Tree Structures

The experiences continued, and I was more aware than I had ever been before. My senses were heightened and on full alert. I would find large, purposely made stick structures that were not accidental. Some with whole, large trees that would be impossible for any human to lift. Let alone carry and stack and weave together as these structures were. The following are a few examples of some tree structures we found.

This tree structure was made by breaking one tree over and bowing another over it, weaving both together with vines and other branches. Then limbs were woven together so tightly it made an immovable "wall". This structure was so sturdy, it could not be shaken or moved at all. Notice the two sticks on

the right side of the first photo. They were simply shoved into the ground.

This is the other side of this particular structure.

This structure was one of significant importance to me. It was the structure where we were introduced to our first bigfoot friend. He made contact with us here at this very spot. I will tell that story later on, devoting a chapter solely to him and his family.

The following is an example of a very large structure made by bowing many trees together and weaving them together at the top to hold it securely.

Next, we have a structure made with entire tree trunks. No human could possibly lift these to construct such a structure.

Why they do this is anybody's guess. It could mark a territory. It could be communication of some sort. We also have the big X formations. It has been concluded by some that the X is a welcome sign. That they are saying "We live here. Welcome." like we as humans lay out a welcome mat at our front door. The following are a couple of examples.

This X was made by wedging & weaving an entire tree between other trees to hold it in place. It was placed.

Right beside the previous X structure, we found another

oddity. A "barrier" of sorts. We saw a stick about 15 feet long placed into two cedar trees

that blocked a pathway going into the woods. I saw this as "Don't go into this area."

We found other various structures as well. Here is one found at one of my research areas.

Another view of this structure. It has two trees that are bowed in opposite directions, and each side is anchored by other branches. There are also sticks placed in the center.

The ends of each side were anchored down with other branches.

Then, there were others. These are a very few of them.

Notice how all these limbs are attached at the top and one is placed horizontally through the middle of them.

Then there are the sticks that are simply shoved into the ground. Here is an example.

While photographing this, I felt a THUMP on top of my head. I screamed for Eric to look to see if anything was on my head.

There was nothing there. After learning more through the years, I now know I was probably being touched by Bigfoot.

Another broken stick nearby shoved deep into the ground.

There are many more examples. These are a few.

This next X structure consisted of a tall tree that was rooted and another large limb that had been carried and placed in that position.

We accidentally knocked this down, & we hastily put it back up. The limb that had been placed there had an odd notch in it that was hooked around the other one to hold it in place. Here is a close up. This next photo is what I see every morning as the sun rises over the mountain.

It is an archway. I believe this may be a portal which my Forest Friends use to visit me. I have captured pictures of them behind my house more than once. I will get into that a bit later.

What is the purpose of these structures? Why do the Forest People make them? I guess we may never know. But I do know that they do make them. These photos show but a select handful of them. If they are important to the Forest People, I'd suggest we pay attention to them and be respectful as we investigate further. Respect is key.

Chapter 16

Rocks, Rocks and More Rocks

Why are rocks so important? I do not know. But just as tree structures are important to the Forest People, rocks seem to be as well. I'd suggest that we pay attention to this if we want to learn anything about them. They hold a significance with them, and there is a reason that they use them to communicate and as well as for other purposes.

What is a rock? It is part of the earth. It is the basic unit by which the earth is composed. It is also part of the trinity "Earth, water and air". This is not a religious symbol to them, but it represents something similar. It is life to them as they know it and their view of life is in its purest, raw form. All things need air, water, and the earth to exist. Therefore, rocks hold a significant value to them.

These Forest People use rocks in many ways. I have found rock stacks in my research areas. Some are made with small rocks. Some are made with very large rocks. Here is an example of a rock stack found at the very spot we heard the loud "tornado siren" call. It was almost impossible to get to it because of the large boulders in the way.

These rocks are so large, it would be almost impossible for anyone to construct this.

I have found many rock stacks. Most are in areas people do not go to. I could bore you to death with multiple photos of them, but I believe I will move on.

The Forest People also gift rocks. Here are a few that were left for me along with a few other things on a gifting rock that I established with them. I believe these

were gifted to me as tools. Sharp flint rocks used for cutting as the Native Americans used. Notice the one rock that has been colored on with a crayon that I left for them. The marbles were brought back to me after being taken, and the weed eater string was tied into a loop. All these objects are now in a shadow box. I am very proud of and cherish these gifts from the Forest People.

Just as I have been gifted rocks in my research areas, I have also been gifted rocks at home. I was building a deck and a staircase at one point. The day after starting all this work, I was given a rock on the new deck of my cabin. What is the significance or purpose of this?

Rocks are occasionally tossed in my direction, towards me and others who are with me, while we are observing other things. I believe they use this as a "Hello! We are here with you!" Not as them trying to hurl rocks at us to scare us or to hurt us. One such day, my granddaughter Aubree and I were looking at odd rock patterns on the side of the road. There were large slabs of solid rock. On these solid rock slabs were rocks that appeared to be placed in a specific pattern. It looked to us like communication of

some sort. As we looked at some of them

These are some of the rocks we were looking at on the slabs of solid rock. It appeared to be some sort of excrement with a circle of rocks placed around it. Other rocks were placed in a straight line.

and got back into the truck, we heard a big "Clunk!" on the roof of the truck. I saw a rock bounce off of the top of the truck and bounce out in front of it. I saw the rock and knew what it looked like. A rock was thrown at the truck! We got out and picked up that rock. It was the same kind of rock that was on the big slabs. These rocks were different than the rocks on the road. They were orange and black. Not like the other rocks that were on the road.

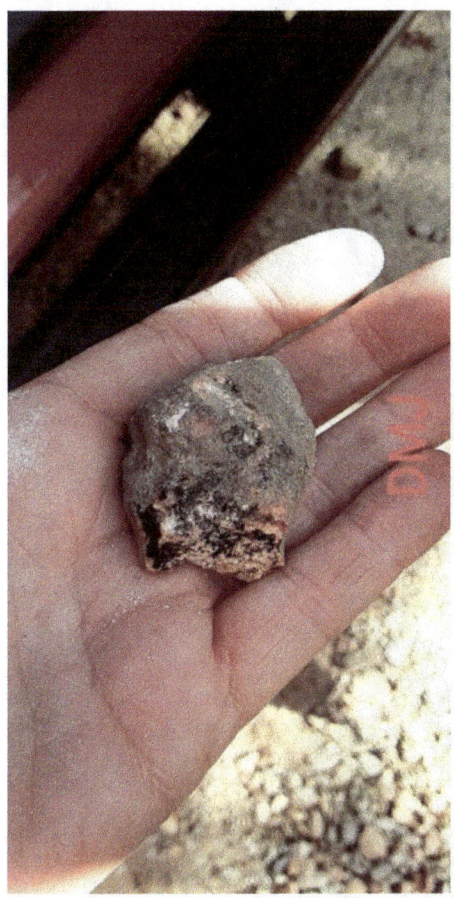

Here is a photo of the rock that was thrown. Notice how it is broken after hitting the truck. This rock matched the rocks on the side of the road but did not match the rocks that were on the road.

Did we snoop a little too much at their rock placements or were they just letting us know they were there? We definitely knew they were there. So, we apologized for being nosey, just in case, and we left that area. I believe those rocks were messages for other Forest people, but I do not know what that message was.

Now we have a strange and unusual thing that was found by my granddaughter Aubree. It was a rock balanced in a tree.

Then we found three other rocks that were placed up high on a ledge. Here, Eric is pointing at the rocks which would be about 10 or 11 feet high. How and why were these rocks placed here? This was at the mouth of a cave. May we go so far as to say this was their way of telling others this cave was already occupied by 3 individuals? Could be. In my experience, I do know they use them to communicate. However, what they are saying is a different matter. Your guess is as good as mine.

Now we come to the rock balancing that I encountered at a specific place. Each day that I crossed this way, I would find two large rocks

that were standing on end. Here is how I found them one day.

Notice the rock on the right side is balanced on its end. The one on the left side is lying down. The next day I

passed by them again. This time the smaller rock on the left was balanced on its end and the larger rock on the right side was lying flat.

This Continued as I passed by these rocks each day. Then one day, the big rock on the right had been moved over about 2 feet and was placed on top of another smaller rock. And both were lying down.

What was the significance of these rocks? What purpose did it serve being moved around every day? They alternated from lying down to being balanced on end every other day. It will, at least for now, remain a mystery.

I believe the Forest People use rocks to count as well. To tell how many of them are at an event or a gathering. I have found evidence of this before and documented it.

I have also found what appears to be an ancient grave in one of my research areas. It is a large mound of dirt with enormous boulders stacked in front of the opening. You can see inside that there is a hollow area. Here are some photos of it.

Previous page is a photo of the opening. You can see there is space inside. It is hollowed out like a tomb.

I do not dilly dally around this spot for long. If it is a grave, I want to be respectful. Nearby here as my granddaughter Aubree and I were looking at a very large footprint we found on a steep slope, we had rocks tossed from above us in our direction just to say hello. I believe they watch this area closely.

There is another research area that I frequent. I have seen and heard and often photographed (unknowingly) bigfoot there. As I was there one day, I decided to play a little game with them. I found a unique rock with a swirl on top of it. And a pretty red colored rock. I also had a big shell. There was a downed tree nearby, so I used that for a "table" to place my rocks and shell on. Here is how I left the gifts.

When I returned, the swirl rock was turned around and the red rock was gone. I found a new rock had been added instead and the new rock was placed beside the shell!

It takes hands to do these things!

These are just a few of the things I have learned about how the Forest People use rocks. Though I don't know exactly what all of them mean.

One thing I have learned is that they do use rocks as tools, to communicate with us and each other, to gift and to count.

Chapter 17

Communication - Stick Glyphs

To what extent can you discuss sticks? How much can one really say about sticks? What value do they hold? It is simply a piece of wood that has fallen or been cut from a tree. Something that most people would discard or burn. But the Forest People do not waste anything. Everything they have access to is essential to their survival, including sticks. Seemingly, something we would simply dispose of can be a very useful tool to them.

I began really noticing stick glyphs when I observed patterns repeated over and over. The same patterns were in many different research areas. One in particular was the "Pi" glyph.

Pi has mesmerized mathematicians, for over 4,000 years. It is a number that is infinite, universal, and irrational. The Pi sign is actually a Greek letter resembling our English letter "n" and is the symbol used to represent the constant. The ratio of the circumference of a circle to its diameter. Pi is infinite.

I once heard that the Forest People see things differently than we do. That "We are all one. Everything is connected. God/Creator, man and earth are all connected." When it all boils down to it, every speck of dust is part of the whole, as we all are. So, this "infinite circle" must be very important, and I decided I should start paying closer attention. After all, they are the teachers.

Here are a few examples of Pi glyphs that I have found over the years. Each of these were found in different areas. This is what piqued my curiosity.

And they were very obvious, meaning they had been purposely placed on a trail or just off of a trail for others to see. Here are a few other examples.

If you look closely there is more than one Pi symbol in this one

This one included other messages along with the Pi .

This one incorporated other messages along with the Pi

symbol. This one seems to be saying A LOT.

Some stick glyphs are blaringly obvious. You see them and recognize that someone is trying to communicate a message with others. The next ones that are pictured are such ones that I found in an area that I had never explored before. The population of this area is 9. The use of sticks and rocks together was amazing. And I discovered 16 inch footprints a few feet away by a stream which solidified these for me. Notice how there are rocks

placed in integral spots in this one.

Rocks marked by me to show placement.

Also, beside this intricate glyph were others as well.

Notice the "Y" stick with a rock beside it.

To

me, this appears to be a signature. The "author" of the glyph

This may not look like a lot, but in an open grassy area it

appears to be a message. It was alongside the previous few.

Marked by me to show placement. Various rocks placed in certain spots alongside the sticks.

These glyphs appear to be messages to others. What they are saying is another story. I'd dare venture to say maybe they are relating who it was that left the glyph (the signature) along with how many were with them or maybe even the direction that they went or their location.

Speaking of location, I have also found a few obvious glyphs that simply point the way. Here are a couple of examples.

Another arrow

Traced by me to show placement

Some glyphs are not so obvious. This is one such

glyph. It was laying in the center of the trail that I used to get to another research area. I am convinced that they see me walking these trails and place these messages here for me to find. The next few were found in the same area.

Notice mostly white rocks are used and the "X" was made from sticks.

I actually have a story about what happened as I was observing these glyphs. But I hate to "jump the gun" so to speak and tell it in this chapter. I will include it later on in another chapter.

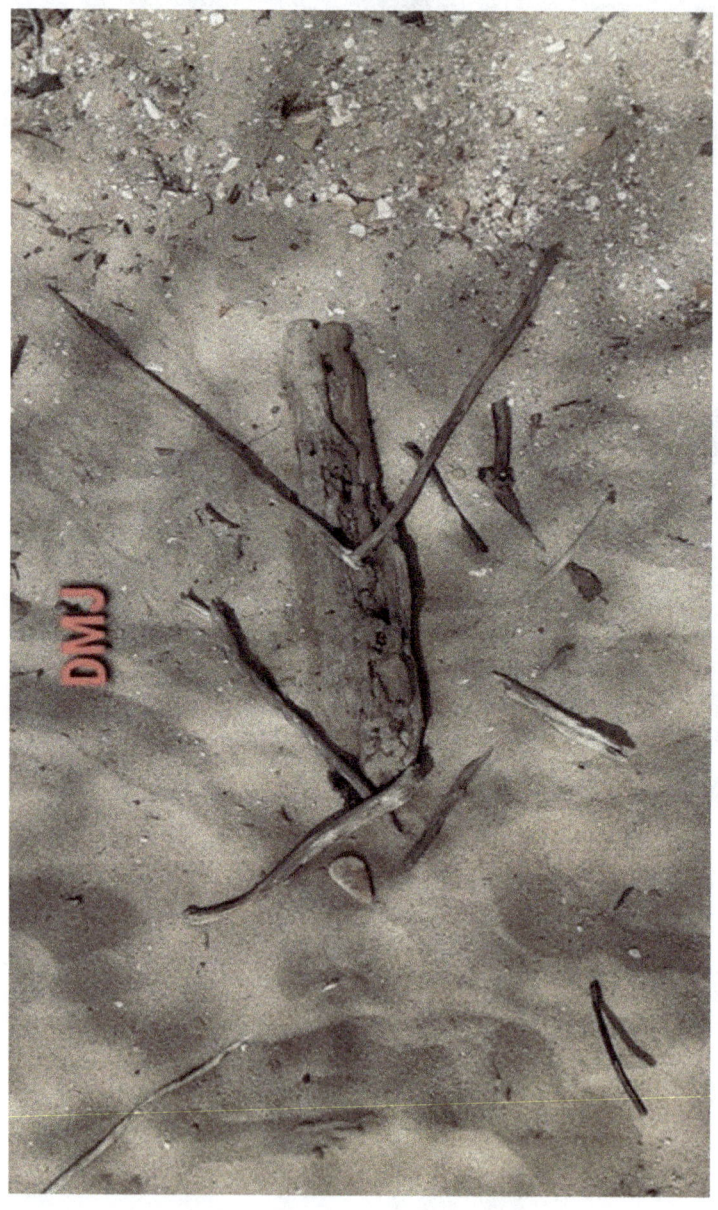

These were intricate glyphs. Not accidental at all. This one contained what some others have observed as well. They call them "stickmen."

Notice the stickman in the center surrounded by "X's"

Then there are the hooks. I started looking into the Rune charts when I started finding these. Runes were used by ancient people to contact the dead, for protection, good luck, and safety. They were used for divination and as a means of contacting other planes of existence.

According to Wikipedia, the three best-known runic alphabets are the Elder Futhark (AD 150-800) The Anglo-Saxon Futhorc (800-1100) and the Younger Futhark (800-1100) The Younger Futhark developed further into the Medieval runes (1100–1500), and the Dalecarlian runes (c. 1500–1800).

The Vikings used letters they called runes. They are imitations of the Latin letters used in most of Europe during the Viking era. It was a way of communicating. Each symbol has a deeper meaning above and beyond what its sound makes.

I was finding similarities between the stick glyphs I was finding and the Rune charts. This hook I kept finding had me

L = ↑ Laguz Water
Fertility, Living Renewal

puzzled. One of my friends, Dorraine, kept finding these as well. We both always found them near water. The following is what I found on the Rune chart.

Next are a few examples of these hooks I discovered. All were within mere feet of the river.

Notice the one on the next page has other features as well as the hook and a rock is placed there on the left as well.

It is important to note that the direction that the hook is placed does not make any difference. I was beginning to realize that the Forest People use many different forms of communication amongst themselves and also as they try to communicate with us as well. So, I started paying closer attention and began looking for these things, these rune symbols, in my yard and all around my house.

Each day as I wake up, I open my back door, which is surrounded by trees, and I say "Hello my friends" to them. I started finding different things on my back deck. There was once the tip of a fern back there with another stick and a couple other things. There are no ferns anywhere near my house. Nor do I own any ferns.

I decided to look up if there was any symbolism of ferns. This is what I found.

> Ferns are often thought to symbolize invisibility, precognition, wealth, and love due to their ancient origins and unique reproductive process.

Well, isn't that a coincidence? It symbolizes invisibility and foreknowledge of an event,

pre·cog·ni·tion
/ˌprēkägˈniSH(ə)n/

<u>foreknowledge</u> of an event, especially foreknowledge of a <u>paranormal</u> kind.

especially of the paranormal kind! Which is right up my alley! I have many different photos of glyphs that were left for me on my back porch, but I won't bore you with all of them. I could go on and on about the Y glyphs and the X glyphs. The Y glyphs are a symbol of friendship. Man, and Sasquatch living side by side as friends. The X symbolizes "We are here" or they are also sometimes left as a gift. Here is such a one that I found in my yard the next day after hearing whistling and finding footprints in my yard one night. I can go on and on about these

because I find many, and I am gifted many.

This is basic, rudimentary knowledge and is widely accepted by most researchers as having a universal meaning. Let's keep moving on to more interesting subjects…

Chapter 18

The Meeting – Urijah and Family

I want to do this chapter justice. No, I want to do my friend Urijah and his family justice in this chapter. This is one of the most important chapters that I will write in this entire book. I need to proceed with the utmost respect for him and his family. They are the focus of this chapter, and I will proceed with all reverence to him, and his family. I'm sure they approve of what I am about to share with all of you as they are the ones who have shared these things with me and taught me over the years. They know what I share with my followers on Facebook. The things they allow me to see and find are what I'm allowed by them to show and reveal to others. They, not me, are in control. There were things they didn't allow me to show, and these things were taken away from me. I saw it but wasn't allowed to share it. It was on my camera. I had it saved in more than one place, and it simply vanished. More about that later on.

Not to sound arrogant, but they trust me. I am a "messenger" for them to get the truth about who they really are out there to the public. They can read a person's heart. They know your intentions. If you are truly there to learn and don't have an agenda, they will teach you many things. But don't expect it to fall into your lap all at once. They, unlike us humans, have more patience than Job. There are times I am shown something, and I don't understand what it is. Then maybe a month later or maybe even years later "DING DING DING!" I realize all of a sudden what they were trying to teach me. They won't shove it down your throat. They wait for you to learn. To accept what your mind will allow you to accept, a little at a time.

First of all, I will tell you that I am one of the humblest people you will ever meet. I do not brag about anything (unless it is my children or grandchildren!) I do not try to exalt myself. I am so down to earth you wouldn't believe it. I don't like attention or being in the limelight. I have been invited to be on tv shows and podcasts and other things. I have turned all of them down. I like to stay in my own little world and keep to myself. I do, however, share what I find on my Facebook page, and I have gained quite a following. I do appreciate all of my followers very much. But I don't like to be in the spotlight. I feel uncomfortable when others praise me for anything. I don't take compliments very well. After all, I am not the one doing any of this. I am simply showing what is revealed to me and what they allow me to share with everyone else. Remember, it is all of them, and none of me.

I feel that is probably the reason the Forest People feel that they can communicate with me. They feel "safe" as well, knowing that I will protect them from any harm, not revealing their location to others. I only show what they share with me. So, as I proceed, I hope I do them justice and share with all of you what they wish to be revealed.

My introduction to this family began when we were walking along through the woods in one of my (now) research areas. I was walking along filming as I went, and I suddenly saw a large, dark figure standing back in the distance. It was humanoid in shape. But it was very large. It was dark and uniform in color. A very dark gray to blackish color. I took screenshots from that video, and I will share them with you.

This is the original screenshot I took from approximately 250 feet away. Keep in mind that I am using my phone to take this video.

Later a friend of mine zoomed into the video and sent me this photo. You can see a large head and very large dark eyes. You can see an extremely long arm, hand, and fingers on the right side. You can see chest muscles. And you can also see it is carrying something on its back. It appears to be a little "something". A miniature of itself.

I traced around the second photo and dotted the eyes for reference to help you if you don't see what I'm seeing. Notice also very broad shoulders & no neck.

Very blurry because it was taken from a moving video and zoomed in about 8000 percent, but you can still see there is something standing there.

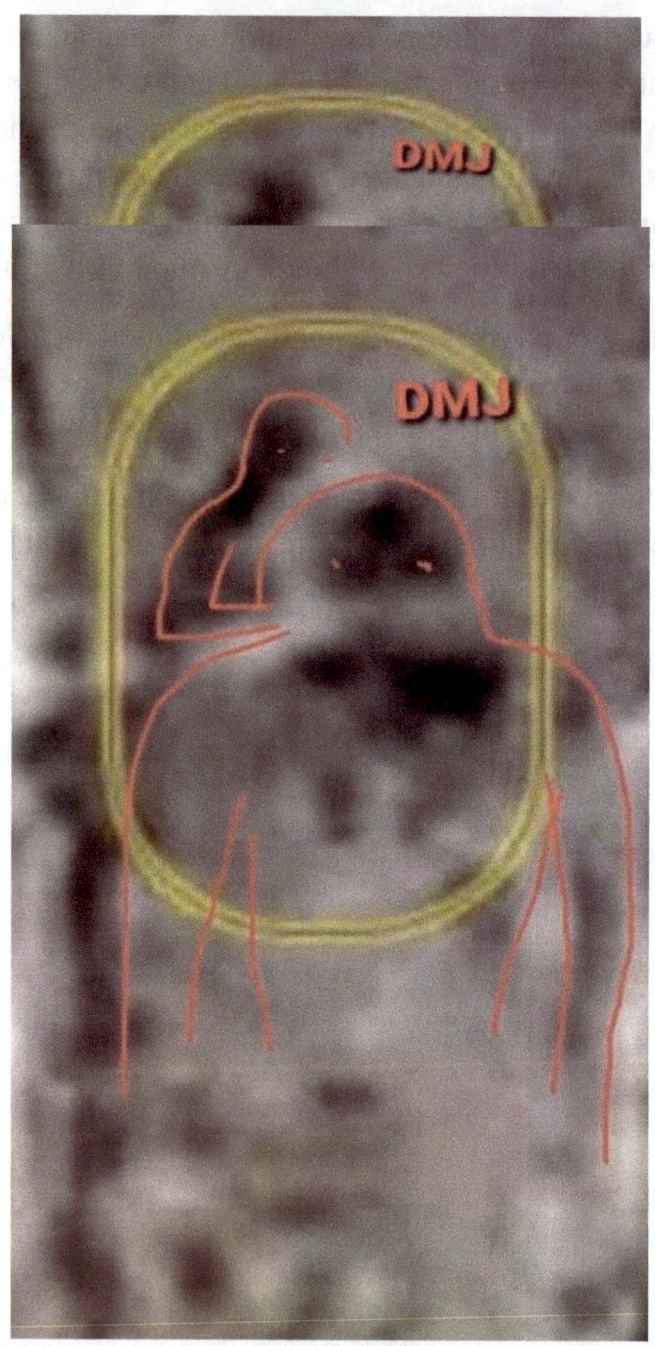

Traced by me and eyes dotted for reference. Notice the little "something" on his back.

Yes, this picture is blurry. It was from my phone camera video zoomed as close as I could get to it at the time which radically distorts the picture. Then my friend took a screenshot from the moving video and zoomed in to the figure as close as he could get which pixelates it even more. But you can still make out the figure and the little one on his back. If you look closely at the first photo, you can even see the little one's eyes as well.

As we approached this dark figure, it ran away, and we heard two loud distinct tree knocks. Was this because there were 2 people there? Do 2 knocks mean there are 2 people there? A warning of sorts to the other Sasquatch People? Later, when we were leaving, we saw the probable reason that they were out there. We saw about 15 deer there lying in the grass. I believe they were there to get their next meal for the family. I filmed the entire event and have posted the video for all to see on Facebook. It is public and anyone is welcome to watch it. This was the first time we ever came face to face with Urijah and Timothy. We didn't know their names at the time but were soon to learn them. This was actually the third thing we experienced here at what I now call "Footprint Alley". But it was the first **visual** that we had of them. This was in February 2019.

The first thing that we noticed at this location happened about a week prior to this sighting. We found a large tree structure that I previously shared with you in Chapter 15. It was beautiful! I was so excited to discover it! I was amazed at how all these limbs were placed and woven together and how there were also two trees used in constructing the frame for it. One tree was bowed over and weaved into the whole and also a tree was snapped over and weaved into the mix. Other branches were then woven on one side together so tightly it was an "immovable" wall. There were 2 sticks on the right that were simply shoved into the ground. It was the most beautiful structure I had ever seen!

View of the other side.

I began to inspect it a bit closer. I knew it was not a man-made structure. There were other things around it that alerted me. Large footprints were in the area around this structure. They were approximately 16 to 18 inches long. So, I began trying to communicate with whoever or whatever made this structure.

Then in March of 2019, even though I felt pretty silly, I started speaking out loud to whomever was there that I could not see. I introduced myself and my husband. I told them our names and I asked what their names were. Of course, we heard and saw nothing. So, we decided to put a notebook into a Ziplock bag to protect it from the weather. I wrote "Hello Friends" in different colored crayons with a big heart under that. Then I wrote "We Love You" with a smiley face. I added some marbles, crayons, a pencil, and a marker to the bag. I showed them how to

use the crayons and the pencil etc. and I left an apple and an apple pie there as well. I placed this at the foot of the big stick structure that we found. When we returned, the apple was gone, and the apple pie wrapper was found about 50 feet away. It had been carefully TORN open. Not chewed open or clawed.

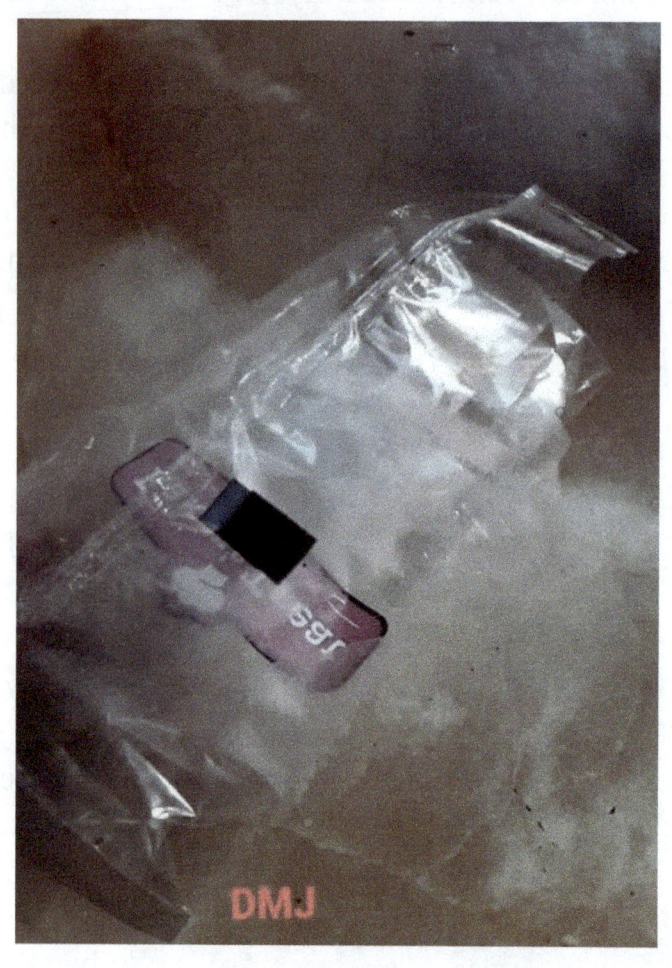

Torn wrapper

The page on the notebook had mud on it. It also looked like fingerprints on it.

Muddy fingerprints on the paper

Also, the way the mud was smeared on the page made it appear as if they were trying to "draw" themselves on the page, using my smiley face for their face.

This is the part that looked like a self-portrait.

Traced by me for reference

I also found some scribble marks with the pencil.

So, I tore that page off of the notebook and wrote another message asking for their name. I also wrote our names on the page. A girl stick figure beside my name and a boy stick figure next to Eric's. We returned to check it the next day and the notebook was still the same. But about

40 feet away in a sandy spot, we found "URIJAH" written on the ground in about 2-foot-tall capital letters, along with a weird star symbol beside it. I now know that the star symbol is called an asterisk, and the Sasquatch People use this symbol frequently. I also did not know what Urijah meant. Was it a word in another language? I documented by taking photos of what I found.

We found URIJAH written on the sandy spot near the tree structure.

This asterisk was there on the end of Urijah. I could not get it all in one photo too easily.

I had no idea what this was when I was there, but thankfully I photographed it anyway. I later learned it was an asterisk, used by the Sasquatch people often.

Footprint found beside the name and asterisk. Notice the bulge on the side of the foot. And remember, this is in chilly March weather. I was wearing a coat and boots.

I wanted to see if I could find out what Urijah meant. So, when I returned home, I did what we all do, and I googled it. I found out that Urijah is an ancient Hebrew name meaning "God is my light". I was blown away! I realized right then, the Sasquatch People are not just some sort of ape. These are very intelligent beings, and I was determined to learn more about them.

As time went on, I kept discovering evidence of them being in the area. Footprints and tree structures. I found a new location close by Footprint Alley and I began to leave them gifts on a big rock I found there. I would leave them apples, marbles, granola bars, nuts etc. Occasionally, they would give me gifts in return. Rocks, footprints, flowers and even a vase were left for me. Sometimes we would place apples along with cherry pies in a tree there that had a small, broken branch which was about 8 feet off the ground. We tied fishing line to the broken branch and added a swivel clasp to the end of it. That branch would not have held the weight of an animal because it would have broken and fallen to the ground. It wouldn't even hold the weight of a squirrel. Anything bigger than a squirrel would have most definitely break

off the skinny, dangling limb. We returned a couple of days later and the pie was gone. I think they love those pies a lot more than the fruit we put out. They didn't touch the apple that time.

Apple and cherry pie hanging from fishing line 8 feet up off the ground.

The cherry pie was gone the next time we checked, but the apple remained.

This happened frequently. Seems our Forest Friends have a sweet tooth. I would usually find the wrappers down at the bottom of the mountain carefully torn open. Not chewed open. That food was inaccessible to animals. The dangling branch would have fallen if an animal had gotten on it. Our Friends did, however, take the apples when I didn't leave other things like sweets.

Nearby, here in the woods, there is a cemetery. There is a trash pile at this cemetery down at the bottom of the mountain where flowers are discarded as well as other things. Right beside the discarded flowers and such things is a huge mound of dirt. I have found their footprints on this mound more than once. Even in 20-degree temperatures. I have named this area Dead Man's Mountain because of this cemetery.

When we first started visiting this spot, we were always greeted with a lot of "whoops". This sounded a lot like what you would hear at the zoo in a chimpanzee exhibit. Sometimes it would sound almost like barking. I believe they were saying hello and also letting the others in the vicinity know that we were there.

I began leaving gifts at a big rock that I found there as I said before. I would usually leave pretty rocks and shells, pinecones, some sweets and or fruit, trinkets like big Christmas bells, mirrors, colorful necklaces, and flowers at times. Here is an example of what I left one day in February of 2020:

I left Reese's candy, colorful rocks, shells, pinecones, sticks and a rubber lizard fishing lure (it did not have hooks in it)

When I returned the next day, everything was the same. Even the Reese's candy was still there. I checked on it every day. That candy and everything stayed the same for many days. Finally, after about 5 or 6 days, the candy and one of the pinecones were gone. There were a few petals from one of the pinecones strewn about and a pile of sharp flint rocks left there in its place. They had gifted me back. I was so excited. Here is how I found the rock when we returned:

Notice the candy is gone and the sharp knifelike flint rocks have been left there on the left side.

On this same day, I checked for any changes at Footprint Alley.

I found a long line drawn on the ground that was about 30 feet long. I followed that line and to my surprise at the end of it, I found 3 drawings on the ground. One was of an apple with little finger marks or a handprint in it. I couldn't visualize what one of them was at the time. And then there was a candy cane looking swirly thing. Here is how I found them all together:

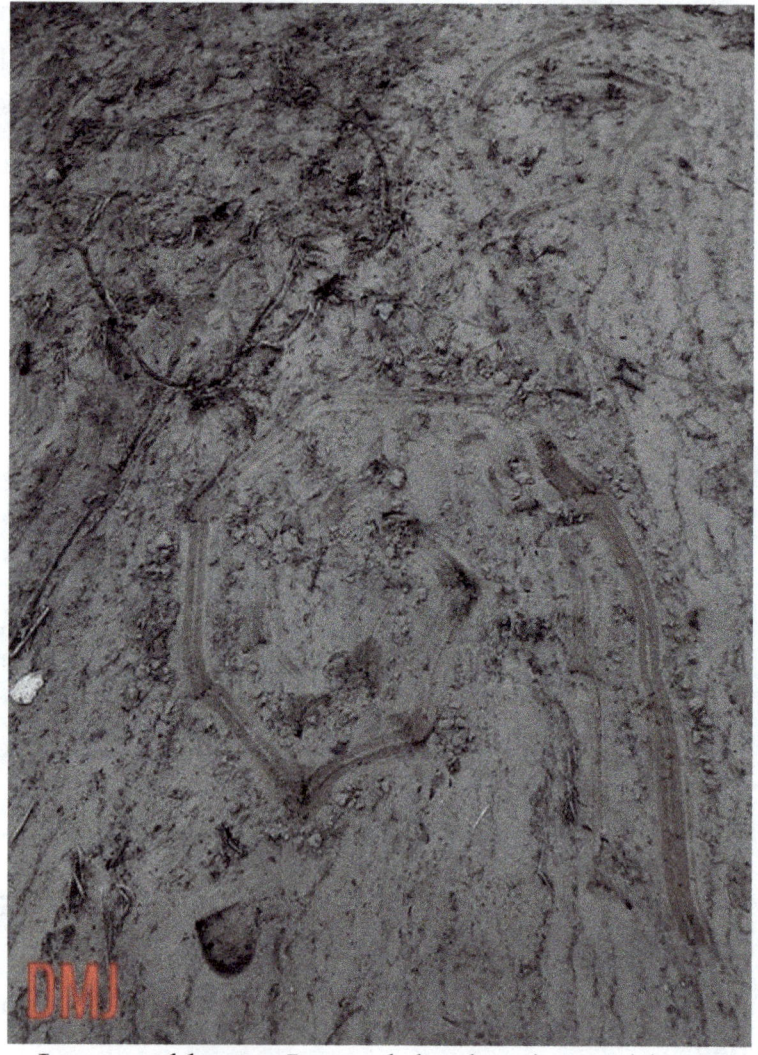

When I returned home, I traced the drawings with my finger so I could see them better. Here is what I found...

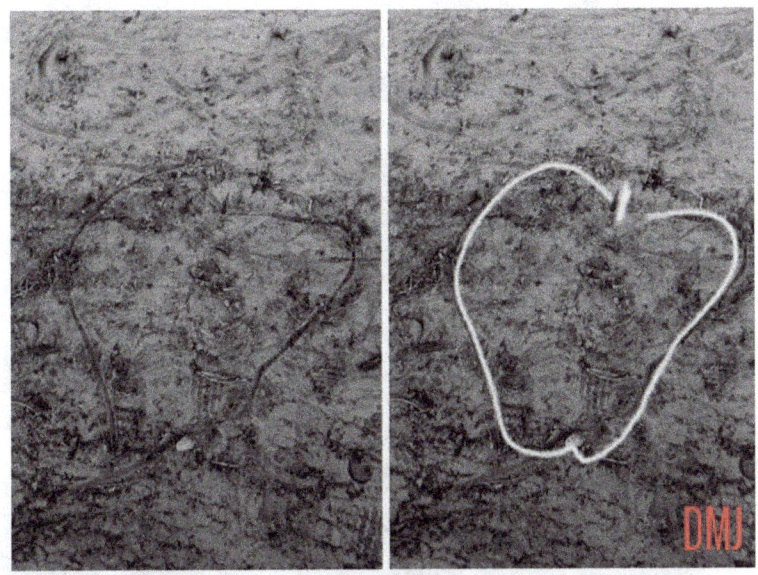

Notice the finger marks or handprint and heart at the bottom of the apple on the left side! And the self-portrait below!

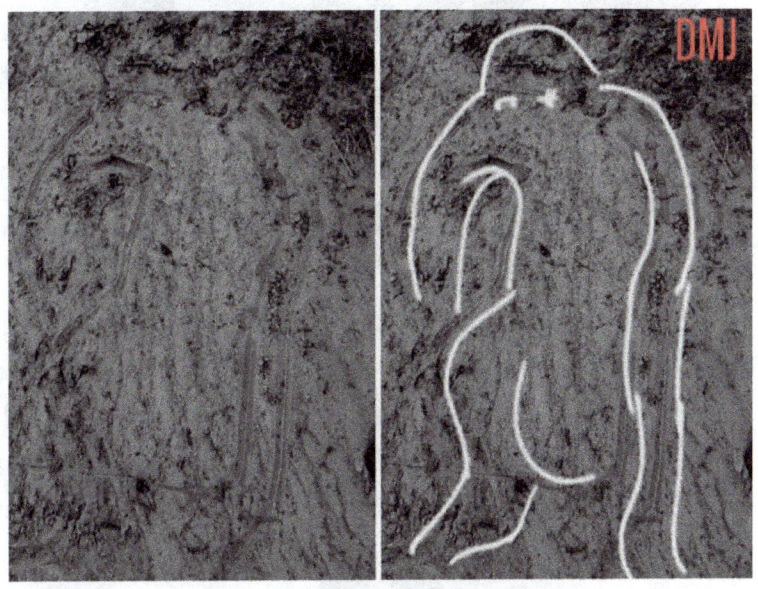

I did not trace the big candy cane looking thing, but it is pretty clear. I later learned this may be a drawing of a portal.

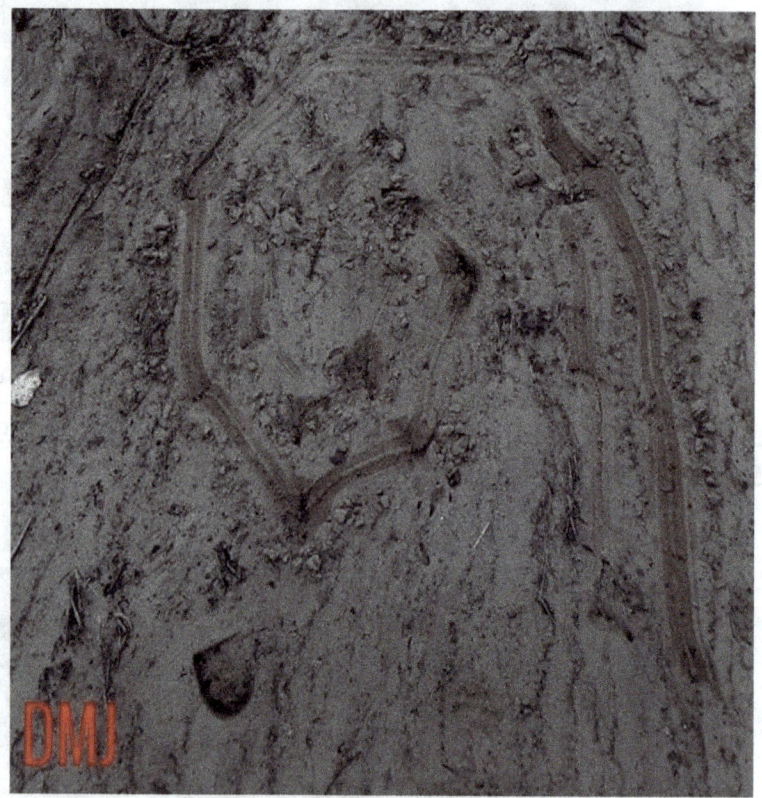

<u>Notice it appears 2 fingers were used to make this</u>

So, the apple was stuck on the end of that very long line. I was putting apples on branches in the trees at Dead Mans Mountain. Was that long line a branch with the apple stuck on the end? Notice also that the apple has a heart drawn inside it and either a handprint or finger marks on it as well.

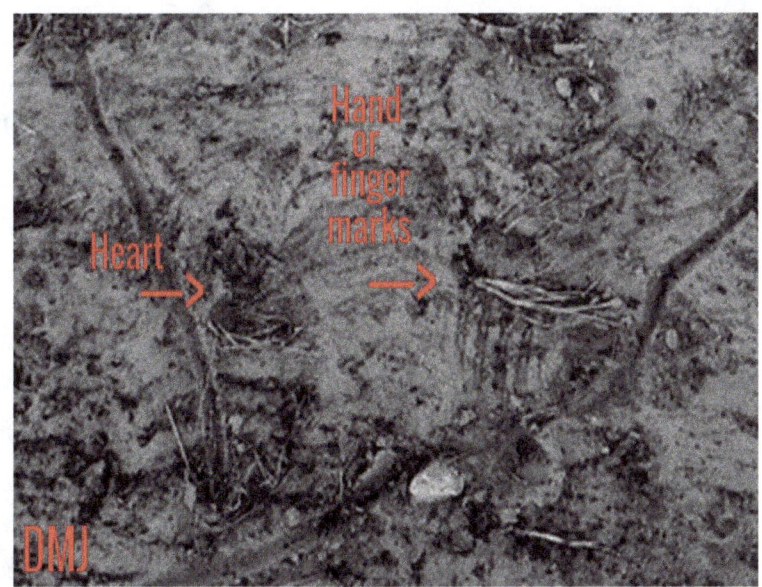

This, I later found out was done by Urijah's little brother Timothy. The way we found out was we always credited Urijah for everything that we found. One day, we found many smaller footprints with Urijah's. And then we saw what seemed unbelievable.

We saw "Hey I'm Timothy" written by these small

footprints. This footprint was in January. It was 20-30 degrees. There would not be a baby out there running around barefooted in the woods. So, we deduced that the small bigfoot on Urijah's back the first time we saw them was Timothy. It seems in my experiences, that an older male Sasquatch is the appointed "babysitter" for the younger ones. That is the case for Urijah and his family here.

I believe that us giving all of our attention to only Urijah made little brother jealous and he wanted to be known. Timothy has drawn us all types of pictures. He loves to make himself known. He is often playing by and in the water, even when there is snow on the ground. The temperatures don't seem to bother the Sasquatch people one bit. Here is another one of Timothy's drawings that includes his face (and it is very accurate by the way) and some footprints. As well as his "signature" which is the little finger marks or handprint. Notice how the signature of the previously shown apple has the same signature as this self-portrait on the next page that he has drawn.

Some of Timothy's artwork

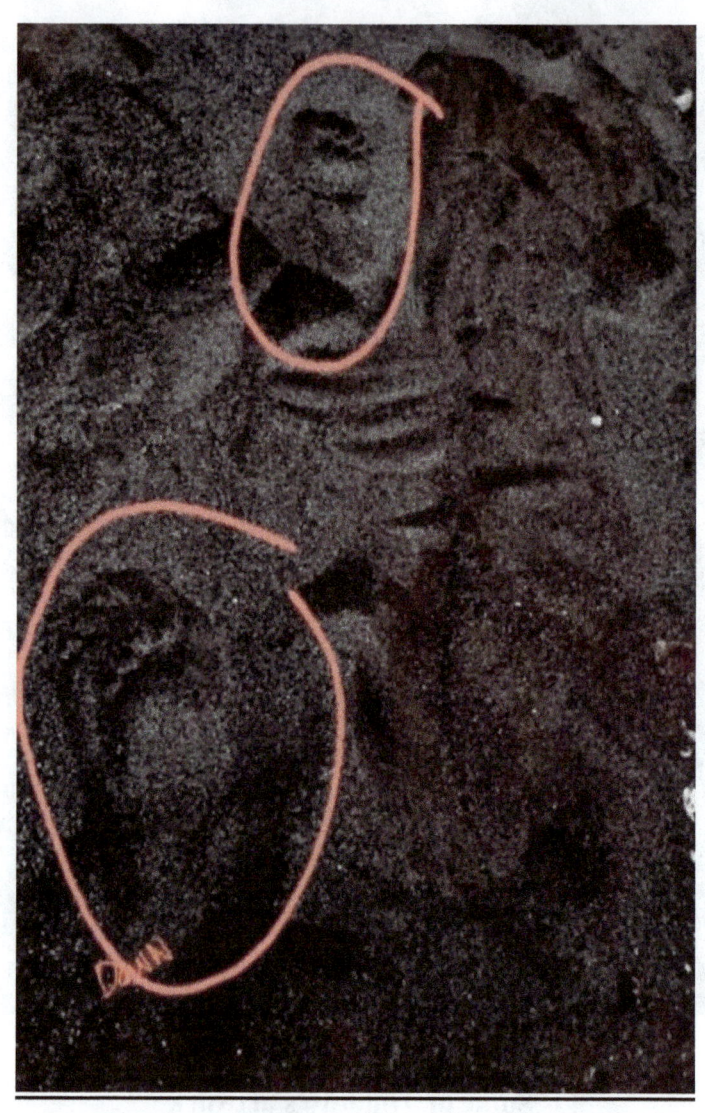

His footprints.

Notice the face there on the right with his "signature" in front of the face. The face is very accurate as to what he looks like as well! He has "droopy" eyes.

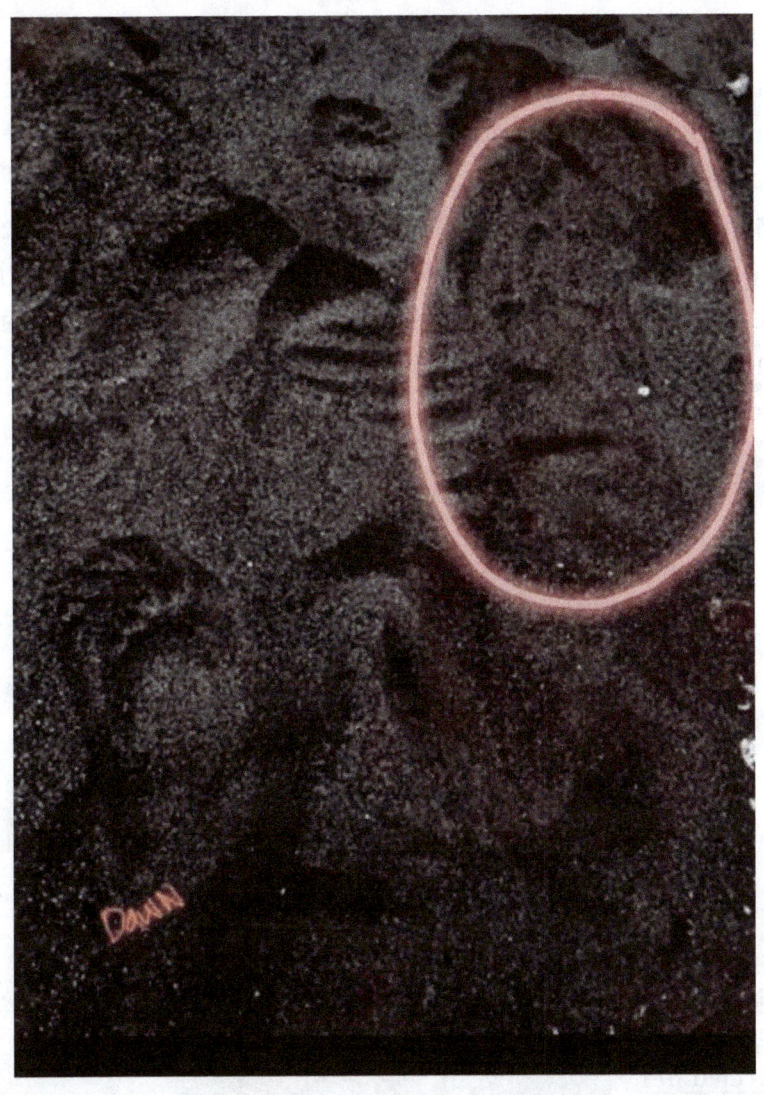

Our little Timothy is very artistic and likes to show his skills. All of these things continued over the next year or so, and we got to be pretty familiar with each other. Then along came little sister.

She introduced herself in very much the same way Timothy did. It was January 2021. I was greeted by a small, what appeared to be a female that I had not previously been aware of. I asked Urijah and Timothy what her name was. The next day I found EDEN written in big letters (the letters were about 2 foot tall each… the same way Urijah was written before) in the sand with a small footprint in it and what appears to be a feather underneath the name.

Feather (?) at the bottom and I circled her footprint.

So now we have 3 members of the family who want our attention. I decided since she was a little girl, I would give her some girly things. I was at one time leaving her shiny beaded necklaces at Dead Mans Mountain and hanging apples in the tree for her. Unbeknownst to me, she was there watching me at the time. I was taking a video of what I was doing and captured her on the video. I took a screenshot from the video. You can see her standing there in the tree line, about center photo, and it appears she had her arms open like she wanted a hug. Here is the first screenshot I took. I zoomed in some and lightened it up quite a bit.

She appears to have her arms stretched out for a hug!

<u>Original screenshot was a bit dark. The apple I was hanging in the tree is at the top.</u>

In the first photo of her, you can see she is female (without going into graphic detail) and she is very bulky. She appears to be between 3-4 foot tall. How sweet it is that she has her arms open like she wants to give me a hug.

Since being introduced to her, I have found that she likes girly things. She also likes suckers.

Previous photo shows a sucker and a necklace I left for her. A year or two later, I found the necklace down at the bottom of the mountain in the area that she plays. It got broken so I left her another one. She also takes the toys I leave her to that same area.

Now that I have talked about the three siblings, I will speak of who I believe to be the mother. I was at the gifting rock one day and I had left something in my truck. I laid my phone down on the rock as I returned to the truck. When I looked through my photos and video 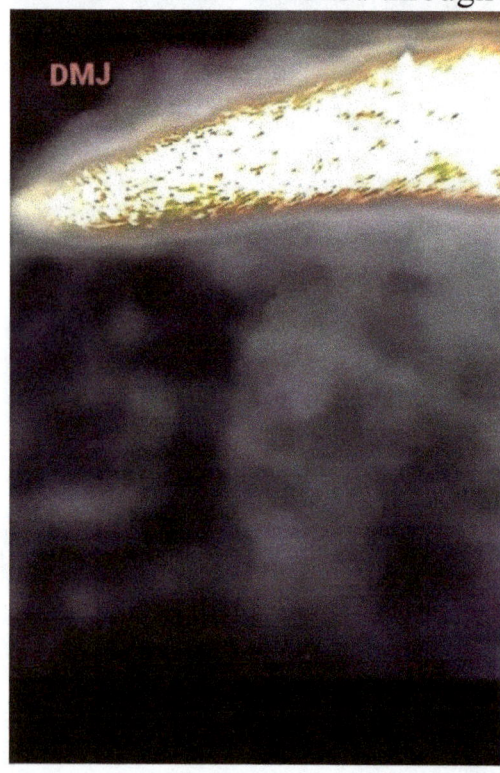 that I took that day documenting what I was doing, I saw a very unusual photo on my camera roll. I see a face on the left. Eyes, nose, and wide mouth (just like Eden's) and a big lower jaw. No hair on the face but it is framed out with hair around it. I believe that golden streak may be one of her hairs, but I may also be wrong.

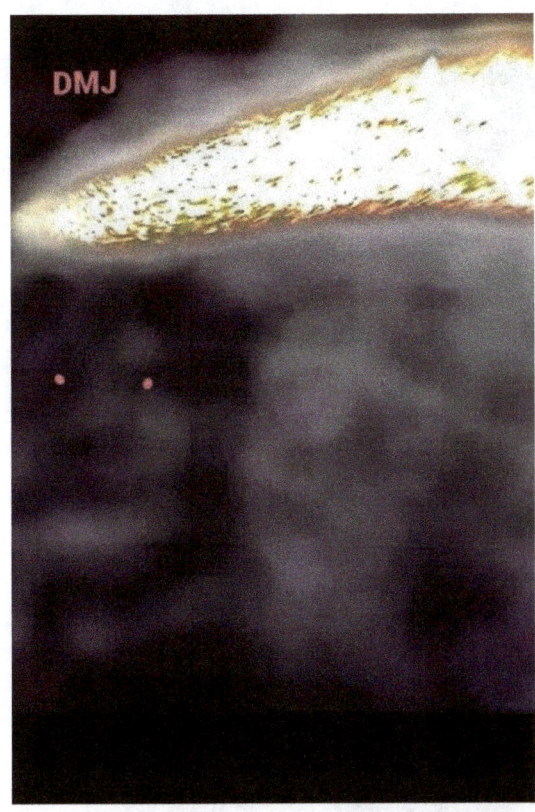

Eyes dotted by me for reference.

When I saw this, it immediately came to my mind that this was the mother. I cannot explain where this message came from. It was like it was told to me, but I didn't hear any voice. I just knew it. She appears to be smiling. How did this photo get on my camera? Was it imprinted by her on there?

And what is that golden streak of light above her head? We may never know but it is evidence to me that these beings are able to do things that we as humans cannot or have lost the ability to do.

Here is a track I found nearby the gifting rock. It was behind a big tree there where they could have easily hidden and watched us.

Traced by me for reference.

You can see the big toe and the outline of the foot. My shoe is almost 10 inches long (women's size 6 Converse) so this track is approximately 15 inches long by 6.5 inches wide. Just amazes me every time I find these things. After all, they don't exist, right?

The more I learned, the more I wanted to know even more. This was stuff out of fantasy. This couldn't be possible. None of this was possible…or was it?

Remember, we are indoctrinated from birth to believe a certain way. Anything outside of that is "impossible." Or is it? It just so happens that if you have an open mind, you might just realize that there is more around you than you have been taught. An open mind is an excellent thing to possess. There are no limits when you open your mind. Not everything is cut and dry.

How else could I explain what I was finding and experiencing? After all, bigfoot is a myth, right? Not so. Now that we know who they are, let's see what else we can learn….

Chapter 19

Just Call Me Arocka

The more things I find, I realize that I am experiencing things that are extraordinary. People don't normally see or find such things as I do. The things I was experiencing were way out of the "norm". How could these things happen and what do they mean?

I don't hardly know where to begin. There was the incident that I mentioned in the last chapter about a video that I took at the large tree structure that we found. It was the first time we saw the structure and I was amazed at its construction. I videoed all around it as I was talking about how sturdy it was and also showed the large footprints we found nearby. Later that day, I posted the video on my Facebook page and in a group. I had it saved on my camera, on my pc and on a flash drive. It had many views and was getting pretty popular. The next thing I knew, it was no longer there. It simply vanished from every place that I had it saved.

Did I accidentally capture something on that video that the Forest people did not want to be seen? How else can I explain this? This is not logical and is a seemingly impossible task to achieve. But it happened. I have no explanation for it. I had to go back and take another video of it. The second one is still viewable.

I have heard that the Sasquatch people can manipulate our electronics and I have had enough occurrences with mine to believe it.

One night, I went to Dead Mans Mountain to see if I could see or hear anything. I do not normally go there in the dark, but I thought I would try it one night. When you are out there, you are very far from any type of light source. It is black as coal out there and you cannot see anything unless you have a flashlight.

I sat in the dark with my video recorder running and the light off. We heard whistling. This was not tree frogs or any type of bird I have ever heard. As a matter of fact, when these whistles began, everything else went silent. You rarely hear birds at night. This was a single, sharp "Whipp!" whistle. One would come from one side of the woods. Then another would answer back from the other side. Then another from a different direction. It sounded like there were about 5 or 6 of them coming from all different directions.

This went on for quite some time. I began making my way down the mountain. I turned on my light for safety to see at that time and the whistles abruptly stopped the moment the light came on. I was about halfway down the mountain when my camera suddenly shut off, and my light went out. I could not see anything. I was in the woods in total darkness and the whistling started up again.

I made my way back up to the top of the mountain a bit shaken. Little did I know that I captured an image on the

video right before it shut down. I posted the video for my friends to see and one of them spotted a face behind the trees smiling at me right before it shut off. She took a screenshot of it and sent it to me. We had to lighten it up a lot to bring out any details. Here is a closer view.

If you look closely, you can see what looks like slanted eyes and even nostrils!

Traced by me for reference.

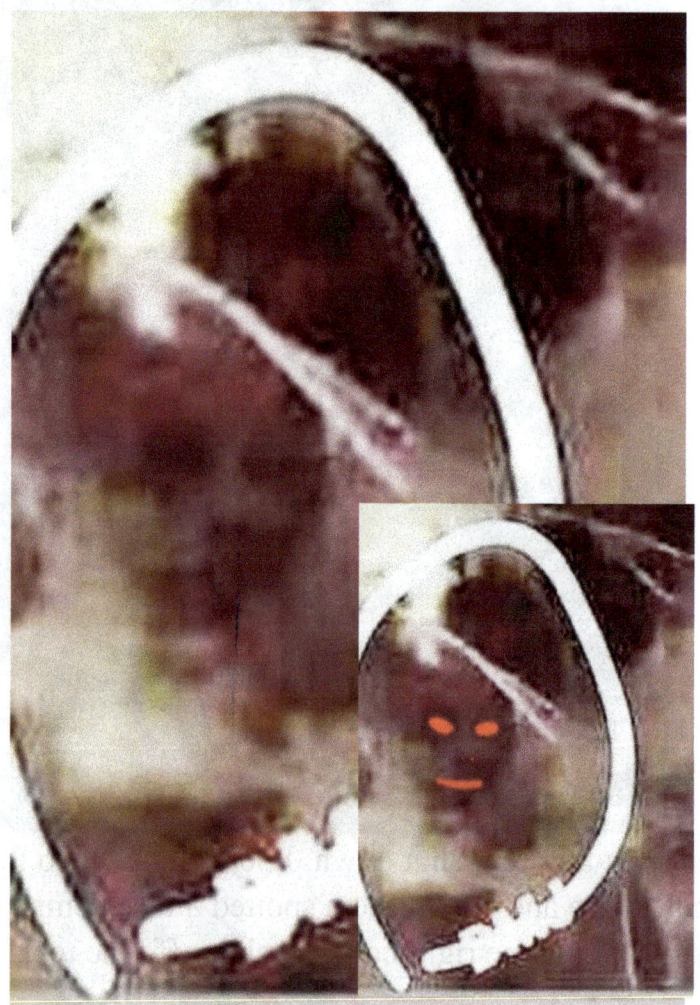

Wow! I was shocked. To have this face peeking through the trees at me at the precise moment my camera and flashlight shut off. What a "coincidence". As I stated before, I don't believe in coincidences.

Since having all of this activity going on that night, I decided to return again at night and try again. I turned on my video camera and began calling my Sasquatch friends. I Called out to Timothy and Eden. I heard the whistles again but not much of anything else. We left thinking we had not captured anything out of the ordinary that night.

The next morning, I listened to what I recorded. Around timestamp 2 minutes into the video, I heard me call for Eden and Timothy. Then I heard what sounded like my own voice slowly say Arocka. What was that? I replayed the video again. I heard myself calling "Eden! Timothy!". Then in what sounded like my own voice slowly say Arocka in broken English. I had no idea what that was.

I could not understand why I heard Arocka or even what that was. And I know I did NOT say it. Then, I had the thought that maybe that was another family member and that they were revealing their name to me using my voice so as not to frighten me. After all, they can do just about anything so why would that be any stretch of the imagination? I thought after all the things I have experienced with the Sasquatch People, nothing seems impossible for them.

So, I went to the old faithful Google search, and I typed in "meaning of the name Arocka". To my surprise, it IS a name, and that name describes me to a tee! Here are some screenshots of what I found:

> **Arocka name personality by numerology**
>
> | | |
> |---|---|
> | **Numerology (Expression Number)** | 22 |
> | **Heart's Desire number** | 8 |
> | **Personality Number** | 5 |
>
> **Talent analysis of Arocka by expression number 22**
>
> *"You are the master builder. You possess a unique gift for perceiving something in the archetypal world - infinite and divine - and making some semblance of it manifest on earth. You dream big. Every goal you have is enormous in scope. You*

You dream big. Every goal you have is enormous in scope. You dream of creating something that will last centuries. Your desire is to change history. You want to make your mark on human civilization. There is no limit to what you are capable of, nor any on what you dream of doing. Of all the numbers, yours possesses the greatest potential for accomplishment."

Inner analysis of Arocka by heart number 8

"You want success in its fullest meaning - wealth, power, and material comforts. You have an enormous ambition. You dream of

<u>Simply amazing! Describes everything about me!</u>

But there is more!

Inner analysis of Arocka by heart number 8

"You want success in its fullest meaning - wealth, power, and material comforts. You have an enormous ambition. You dream of big projects, great undertakings, and rewards. You are a visionary. You see the horizon and the promise. In general, you also see the methods necessary to fulfill that promise. But you are not especially good with details; you need others to help you deal with the smaller parts of the picture."

Information courtesy of nameslook.com

"You are a stimulating person. You brighten social gatherings with your fresh and original ideas. Your conversation tends to be sprinkled with novelty and wit. You have a quick tongue and charisma. You are probably an excellent salesman. There is a lot of nervous energy within you looking for an outlet. You love your freedom and you see this life as an ongoing adventure. You are upbeat and optimistic."

I love to build. I have built a few rooms onto my house and just continue adding on with decks that surround my house. I do have big dreams of doing big things. I have one of opening a Bigfoot Exhibit/ Museum for children. I am always planning and trying to figure out what to build or do next. I am a BIG dreamer. I see no end to what I can do. I can usually figure out a way to do anything that I want to accomplish. I am a nervous type of person who needs to be doing something at all times (nervous energy). And I do need a lot of help with details. I cannot follow written directions at all, so I always need help from others with that. And I am an excellent "salesman" as I started selling when I was a 12-year-old child (door to door Christmas card selling every year). And to this day I have a few online shops where I sell all types of things. Is Arocka the name they are giving me? I certainly think so! You could not explain my entire personality any better than that. Everything is to a TEE.

Now after I found all of this, I replayed the video once again. I heard myself say "Eden! Timothy!" then… silence. That voice, "my" voice, that was there on the video before which said "Arocka" was no longer there. It vanished from the video. I listened to it twice before and it was there. What just happened? It was no longer on the video. That "sealed the deal" for me. I realized they were letting me know what they call me. They named me Arocka.

Remember, they know you better than YOU know you. They can read your every thought and ambition. They know your intentions and what you are all about without you saying a word. So, if you want to connect with them, make sure your intentions are pure.

Moving on now to another wild and crazy but true experience. This took place in July of 2022. In my kitchen, I have what I call a "wall of memories" where I have some of my best and most memorable captures of bigfoot printed and framed. I had some bigfoot collectibles, and I needed a place to display them. So, my husband made a shelf that would hang on the wall. I hung it there on the "wall of memories" and was so pleased with it. I wanted to take pictures of it to show my friends. As I was attempting to get the whole wall with the pictures and the shelf in a photo together, my camera (phone) was suddenly knocked out of my hand and a photo was snapped. It was rather startling to have it knocked out of my hand, but odd things happen to me all the time, so I brushed it off. I did catch my phone before it hit the floor and I took a few other photos of the shelf and wall. When I looked through them to find a good one to share with my friends, I saw that accidental picture that was taken as the camera was knocked out of my hand. I was shocked!

Next, I will show you a cropped part of the accidental picture. I zoomed in closer to see the details and what was in the photo.

Here is a cropped and zoomed in part of that photo:

I see a cone shaped head on the upper left. I see a

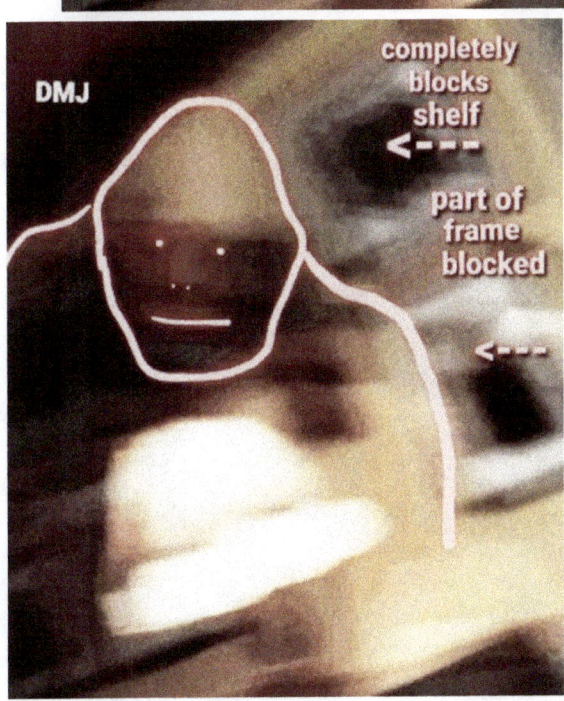

prominent brow ridge, 2 eyes, a nose, and a mouth. Looks as though he even has a light-colored beard. I also see four fingers to the right of the bigfoots face like it is holding something out in front of it. It is completely blocking out the shelf and even part of the picture frame beside it. Traced by me for reference.

Then I also noticed in the uncropped picture, that there was an odd strand of white light close to the center of it.

Here is the uncropped photo. Notice the suspect bigfoot

on the left upper side and the strand of white light closer to the middle of the photo.

What could this be?

I also zoomed in even closer to the suspect bigfoot's face and changed the color to see if we could see anything else. Next is the photo that I turned black and white. You can clearly see his cone shaped head, eyes, nose, and mouth.

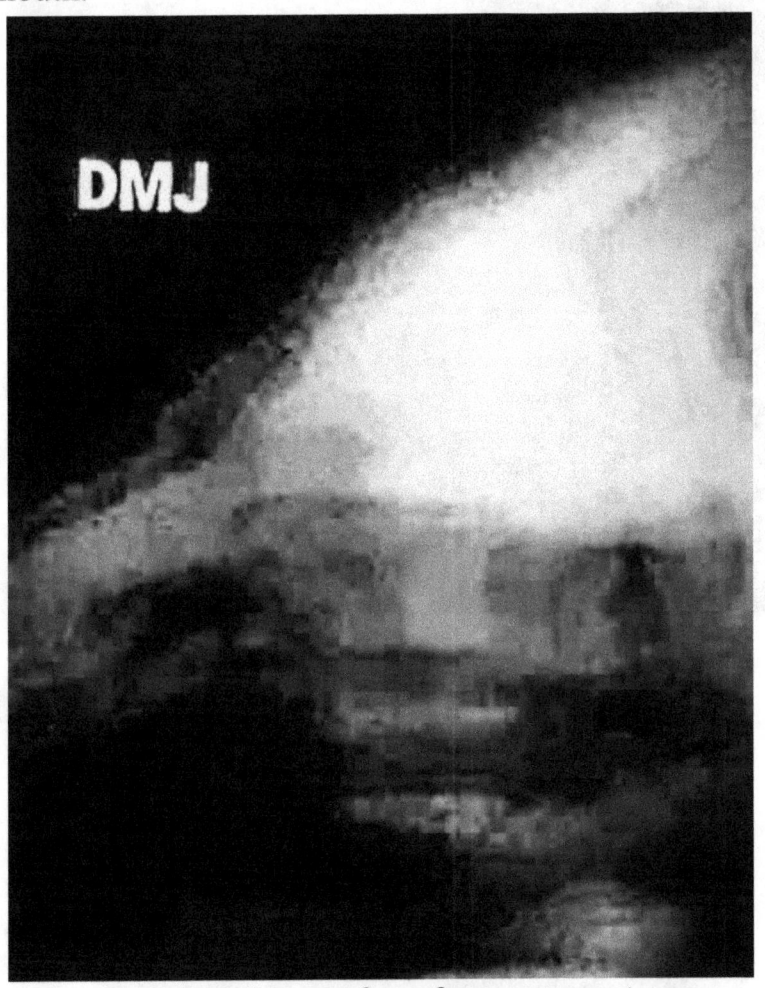

<u>Eyes dotted by me for reference on next page.</u>

This photo shows the final photo I took that was crystal

clear.

I'm simply amazed about this. They can come inside your home. They don't even need to use the door.

I have heard it explained as they operate on a different vibrational frequency than we do. Everything down to a speck of dirt has a vibrational frequency. Tiny vibrating strings of energy make up every particle in the universe. It seems the bigfoot has the ability to change their vibrational frequency so that they can move through solid matter. They can hide in plain sight just by controlling their vibration and seem to simply vanish right in front of your eyes.

I have also been patted on top of the head on different occasions when there was nothing there that I could see. It always happened when I went out to one of my research areas. And I for one have personally witnessed one's "disappearing act".

I watched as a bigfoot ran along the tree line, moving faster than what seemed possible. It was approximately

50 feet from me. I could only see him from the waist up because his legs were "invisible." I had a back/side view. I saw the shape of his head, his massive shoulders and muscular back and all those muscles moving as he ran alongside my truck. He was running smoothly (as if gliding) out in the open with nothing blocking my view of his legs, but they were simply invisible. He didn't bob up and down. Eventually, the rest of him vanished too as if he passed into another dimension. It was very wild!

Another time, Eric and I were visiting Stone Doll Holler. It was in January or February. I was standing out in front of the tree line getting ready to walk in with the gifts that I was going to leave my Friends for the day.

Suddenly, I started feeling a repeated poking on my leg. It was what you would feel if a small child was poking at you trying to get your attention. I was busy gathering the gifts together and wasn't paying a lot of attention. I assumed it was a stick or something blowing around that was poking me.

When I eventually looked down to see what it was, it stopped. There was absolutely nothing near me that I could see. Suddenly, I saw what looked like little footsteps running away from me. I could see the leaves, debris and dirt flying up with each step. But there was nothing visible to make those footsteps. I thought "Wow!" to myself and went on. I didn't tell anyone about it because I thought it sounded too far-fetched for anyone to believe. But later that day, Eric shared something with me that happened to him there that day as well.

He likes to do crafting and he uses small sassafras saplings to make hillbilly pencils. He said every time he would bend over and touch his knife to a sassafras sapling to cut it, something would poke him in the ear. He looked and there was nothing there. There were no insects out because it was way before spring. This happened to him 3 times until he finally gave up and did not cut any of them.

When he told me this, I shared my experience with him as well, knowing he would not think I was off my rocker. Someone was there and wanted to be known. I think it was probably a juvenile just playing games with us. After all, if I had the ability to be invisible, I would have a blast entertaining myself doing such things to unsuspecting people. It would be quite amusing!

I have a Forest Friend whom I have named Flute. I will dedicate an entire chapter to him later on. But he has visited me inside my home as well. He lives approximately 20 miles from my home in one of my research areas.

One morning as I lay there in bed about to get up, I heard him. He makes a sound like a flute, and I will explain all of that in "his" chapter. He made the loud flute sound right beside my bed. I just smiled and said, "Hello Flute."

Another time I saw a silhouette of what appeared to be a bigfoot in my bedroom. My bedroom doors are French doors that have stained glass windows in them. The light from the other window in the bedroom lights up the windows when you are looking at them from the room next to it. I saw the dark silhouette of what appeared to be an approximately 6.5-foot-tall bigfoot through those windows. It was very large and muscular like a football player in his gear with the shoulder pads. When I reached the door and opened it, the shadow ran towards the bathroom in the back of my bedroom, and it was gone. I just said, "Hello Friend" and left it at that. The impression I get is this is a male and is the same one that made his presence known in my kitchen.

Another time, Eric and I were visiting close by one of my research areas. I was walking around photographing a few new footprints. All of the sudden, I started feeling really horrible. I had an immediate headache and my heart started pounding. I could even feel it pounding in the back of my head. I got a sense of dread and doom. I wanted to leave, and I returned to the truck.

At that time, Eric was walking around in the bamboo (cane). This bamboo is tall. I'd estimate it at about 10 to 12 feet tall. He saw some large tree branches about 20 feet in front of him start moving around and then the bamboo in front of that tree started swaying. This was not from the wind. Nothing else was blowing around. He got very spooked. Then he heard what sounded like something large moving around back there and he ran out of the bamboo field and returned to the truck where I was sitting. I told him I wanted to leave, and I didn't feel good.

Later that night, after arriving home, we started talking about what we had found that day. He told me about the tree moving and the bamboo swaying. Then said he immediately felt very bad. His head began throbbing just like mine had. I told him about my experience as well. We concluded that we may had been hit with infrasound. Maybe we were too close to something that they didn't want us to see or that there may have been danger lurking nearby that they were protecting us from. Hitting someone with infrasound would definitely make them want to leave an area.

Infrasound is a real thing. Sound waves of frequency below the range of 20 Hz are called infrasonic sounds. It is not detectable by the human ear. Rhinos, hippos, elephants, whales, octopuses, pigeons, squid, cuttlefish, cod, Guinea fowl, etc. communicate via infrasonic sounds. Tigers use infrasound to communicate over long distances or through dense vegetation. Tigers also use infrasound to paralyze their prey. Humans who hear a tiger roar may also experience a sensation of momentary paralysis.

I do believe bigfoot have the ability to use infrasound. However, they, like the others we know of that use it, are not animals. I do not believe that bigfoot use it as a weapon, but personally speaking, it is effective for avoiding unwanted contact at an inopportune moment. I suspect this is a "tool" they can pull out when needed.

They can add this to all the other abilities they possess, such as vibrational frequency, to remain hidden from humans. How else do you explain how there are so many people who have never visually seen a bigfoot but have unknowingly walked right by them? They felt their presence or heard loud footsteps walking right beside them but never saw anything. How can something that large remain hidden?

It is definitely a mystery, but I am sharing what I have come to know or believe over the last 9 or so years. No one is an expert in this field. It is and will probably always remain a mystery. Especially to those who can't or won't open their mind to the possibility that these beings are not animals or that they have extraordinary abilities that we do not or no longer possess. In my opinion, they are superior to us in every way.

Chapter 20
The Gift Of A Friend

I have been gifted many things from my bigfoot friends. Some people believe that a gift has to be an item that one goes to the store and purchases. The more expensive the gift, the better it is. They don't understand that the best gifts come from someone's heart. It doesn't have to cost a penny to be the most cherished gift to another person. As is the case with the gifts I have received from my Forest Friends. And the gift of their acceptance of me is the best one of all. I will share a few of the others here with you.

One day, I was visiting Dead Man's Mountain. As a matter of fact, it was 2 years ago on this very day…July 14, 2021. I had established a gifting rock there to leave gifts for my Forest Friends, and in time, began receiving gifts from them in return. I visited that day and found a few odd things had been randomly moved or taken away. And there at the foot of the gifting rock, lay a cement vase. This is the type of vase you see in a cemetery on the sides of the tombstone for putting flowers in. It is usually cemented down on the tombstone. I didn't know what to think. I knew there was a trash pile out in the woods at the bottom of this mountain.

The vase was placed on the ground in front of the gifting rock.

I did not want to take it with me! So, I placed it underneath a large bush beside the gifting rock and left it there. I returned sometime later and the sticks that I had laid on the gifting rock had been taken off of it. They were then used to make a large X placed on top of that bush and another stick was pointed straight down and was sitting right on top of that vase. It's as if they were saying "Here is the vase we brought you and you forgot to take it!"

This is the "X" they placed on the top of that bush.

This is where I placed the vase under the bush to hide it.

I reluctantly decided I had better take the vase home with me because they seemed insistent that I do so. I did not want to hurt their feelings. So, I bought some flowers for it and sat it out in my yard. It is a reminder that when they give you something, they expect you to receive it with gratitude and bring it home.

<u>The vase now sits in my yard.</u>

Another gift I received was one which I could not physically bring home with me. On December 21, 2020, we visited one of the research areas I call Stone Doll Holler. This gift is the precise reason that I call it that.

Keep in mind, the temperatures had been in the teens and 20's.

There beside the freezing cold water's edge was a rock art image of myself. It was very intricate using perfectly shaped rocks for the face, lips, eyes, hands, fingers, foot, and toes. They even made the fingers anatomically correct on both hands. Shorter first finger. Longer middle finger then a shorter finger next and lastly the pinky finger shorter. The hair was made with all white rocks (I have blonde hair) It was approximately 3 feet long by about 2 feet wide. Fairly good size.

There were also two footprints approximately 15-20 feet away from this "sculpture". They were also by this freezing cold, spring fed body of water. The water here is like ice even in the summer. One footprint was approximately 15 inches long and there was a smaller one approximately 7 inches long there as well.

As I observed this beautifully made image, from the woods nearby, I heard one single "WHOOP!" It was as if they were saying "Yes, we made that for you." At any rate, this was a treasure to me. I could not take it home with me, but I did take photographs of it. It is now printed and framed on my wall of memories in my house. I will show a few photos of it here:

Notice the "hair rocks" are all white. Also notice the shape of the lips and they even added one pupil in one of the eyes.

Notice the length of the fingers is anatomically correct.

An approximate 15-inch footprint nearby. For reference my shoe is 10 inches.

<u>Another approximate 7-inch track nearby beside the water.</u>

Someone put a great deal of thought and work into creating this for me. I noticed that it wasn't quite complete as it was missing one leg and one pupil. I must have interrupted them as they were finishing it, and they ran for cover in the woods nearby.

It was so thoughtful of them to do this for me and is one of the most cherished gifts I've ever received from them. I tried in vain to create something like that for them, an image of their people, but it was a futile effort. It took me so long to find the perfect rocks that were shaped and colored correctly and the correct size I eventually gave up. It would have taken me at least a full day to do it. But they are very patient in everything they do.

Another gift was given to me on April 12, 2021. I was at another research area. I named it Footprint Alley for a good reason. I regularly find bare footprints here, even in the snow. This is where Urijah, Timothy and Eden play. I had left a written message for them a few days prior on the ground.

When I returned, I found this beautiful piece of driftwood embedded with rocks beside the message I left along with straight line footprints and other things.

Message I left on the ground.

Beautiful piece of driftwood embedded with rocks was left where I had left the message.

Straight line footprints beside the driftwood. These are identifiable as Urijah's because of the size and shape.

<u>Finger marks beside the footprints and driftwood.</u>

More rock art close by.

They are so thoughtful and creative with their gifts! I took the driftwood home with me, and it now sits on a dining table on the back deck. I love Urijah, Timothy, and Eden. They were all young at the time and very eager to communicate with me.

Speaking of rock art sculptures, I have found others similar to that last one that was shown. Here is another one I found on June 11, 2021:

I found this one at the same place I was gifted the driftwood on a different day and the similar rock sculpture. I also found both Urijah and Timothy's footprints here the same day.

Urijah's footprint in 2021 was approximately 10 inches.

And here is Timothy's. His was approximately 8 inches in 2021.

They do have a way of making beautiful art for me to find.

Just up at the top of the mountain from Footprint Alley is Dead Man's Mountain as I told you about earlier. The trash pile of discarded flowers seems to be the place The Forest People like to get gifts for me. On June 11, 2021, as I left Footprint Alley, I decided to check on the gifting rock I had established there with them. I had previously left a purple, beaded necklace, a large red Christmas bell, a piece of weed eater string, some pretty rocks, a "Y" stick, and a rock that said "hope" on it. When I got there, I was pretty surprised by what I found.

The necklace and bell were gone. Some of the smaller rocks were gone. The "Y'" stick was gone. The "Hope" rock had been turned. The other rocks that remained had been moved and the weed eater string was gone. There was a basket of flowers sitting in the spot where the "Y" stick had been. It was a big bouquet. I took a few flowers from that bouquet home with me and thanked them for their kindness. See the next 2 pages for the photos of before and after.

This is how I left it.

This is how I found it. Also notice, the big pink rock has been turned as well

I was gifted 2 more bouquets. I found them May 2023.

Again, here at the same spot in May of 2023, I was gifted 2 more bouquets of flowers.

As I said before, they have gifted me sharp flint rocks here as well. Here is my collection of a few that I was gifted and some marbles that were re-gifted back to me at various times. A small piece of weed eater string that they tied into a loop. And the rock they colored on with the blue crayon I left for them.

Notice the rock that that they colored on. I found it and the broken crayon laying in front of the gifting rock.

This rock is now in my shadow box along with other gifts.

On another occasion at Stone Doll Holler, I was gifted a piece of Charcoal and a sprig of cedar that were left in the fork of a dead tree. This has a story all on its own to go with it which I will share in the next chapter, but I will show you what they left. This dead tree is my gifting spot at that location.

<u>Also, notice the white heart shape on the piece of charcoal.</u>

I don't know where they came up with this charcoal. I suppose they must have visited a campsite. I did a little research about the health benefits of charcoal. I discovered that it is an emergency toxin removal. It flushes out poisons from your body. It helps with digestion. It lowers cholesterol and the list goes on and on. I also looked up the benefits of cedar and found the cedar tree has many practical and medicinal uses. Cedar is offered to the sacred fire during sweat lodge ceremonies, burned during prayers and, when boiled, can purify indoor air, and be used for cedar baths. As a tea, it can help to reduce fevers, rheumatic symptoms and relieve symptoms of chest colds and the flu. What thoughtful gifts of medicine. I eventually took these home with me and labeled them as to when and where I had been gifted them.

They use everything around them. There is no waste. They are masters at using everything around them to survive. They are very wise, and they know exactly what they are doing.

On a side note, before taking the charcoal and cedar sprig home with me I placed a marble on the same tree right beside them. When I returned, the charcoal and the marble were buried together in a hole under the tree. Why would they do this? I left it there for two days. Then, I decided to take the marble, the charcoal, and the cedar sprig home with me. I buried two shiny coins in that same hole there in its place. A new quarter and a new penny. Those coins remained there for a couple of weeks, then they were taken. I hope they liked the trade!

This is how I documented what happened at the gifting tree. I glued them all to this paper and wrote out what occurred. Real location name blotted out for privacy.

These are just a very few gifts I have received from The People of The Forest. There is no way I can include them all.

Chapter 21

My Friend Flute

As I mentioned in the last chapter, the charcoal and the cedar sprig have a story all their own and I will tell you about it in this chapter.

On February 17, 2022, I was at Stone Doll Holler checking for footprints as I found them there occasionally. I didn't have any fresh fruit at home, so I took a pack of peaches to leave as a gift. I had previously established a gifting tree farther back into the woods. We then noticed a random piece of charcoal and a small sprig of cedar had been placed in the fork of a dead tree that had fallen over and was closer to the trail. Where would this charcoal have come from and WHY would it have been placed on this tree?

We then began hearing a noise occasionally. It sounded like a flute. Every time we got close to this charcoal in the tree, we would hear the "flute" sound. If we backed away from the tree, it would stop. You can hear this flute noise on the video I was taking at the time. I had no explanation for this. At times it was a solid "note" and sometimes it would "quiver" at the end of the note. It was very strange.

I was getting a bit alarmed at this point, so we left the peaches on the tree and went back to the truck. As we walked away, we heard the flute sound again and it sounded sorrowful this time. So, I decided to do a little experiment.

I got a blue marble out of the glove box of the truck. I carried these with me to leave as gifts because I have heard that they like marbles. In particular, blue marbles. I wanted to leave this marble as well as the peaches to say thank you for letting us visit their home. We walked back to the tree and just like before, every time we got near the tree, we would hear the flute noise again.

We left the marble there on the tree and walked away. It made the mournful noise again as if it was sad that we were leaving. Quite honestly, I was getting a bit freaked out by this at the time.

I told you in the last chapter what happened with the charcoal and marble being buried together after all of this happened, so I won't bore you with telling it over again. But I didn't understand what was happening.

I watched and rewatched the video that I was taking at the time all of this was occurring, over and over. I was looking for anything out of the ordinary. Trying to see if I could spot the "culprit" anywhere near us. I would watch and if I saw anything odd, I would pause it and take a screenshot from the video.

After reviewing it multiple times and looking through the screenshots, I spotted him! He was across the stream from us on the other side on top of the bluff. He was watching the spot where the charcoal was.

Screenshot showing the tree and his lookout location from the top of the bluff.

Zoomed in a bit more.

Zoomed way in and lightened. You can see his eyes and he has what some call a Jimmy Durante nose. He is peeking over the bluff through the bushes watching us.

Eyes dotted by me for reference.

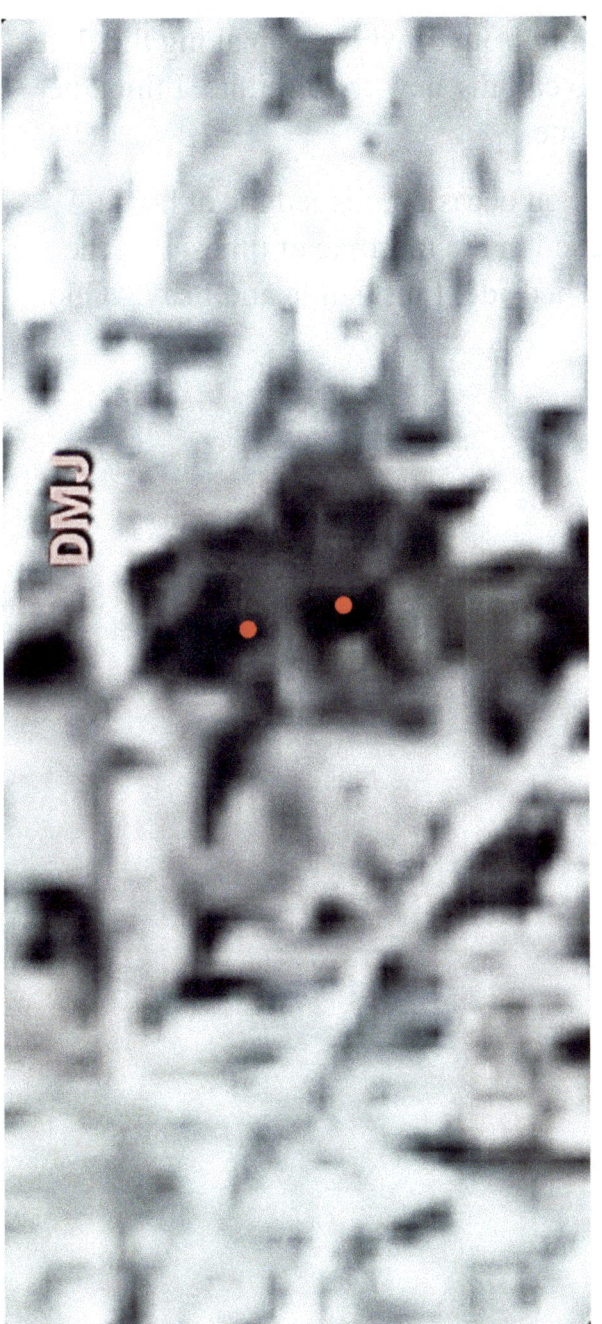

After finally spotting him, my fear was gone. It was just the fact I was hearing something, but I didn't know where it was coming from or who was making the flute noise. I decided to call my new friend Flute. I think he enjoys singing to me.

He has since then, on occasion, visited me at home. I have been awakened in the morning at times with the flute sound at my bedside. I just smile and I say, "Good morning, Flute."

Chapter 22

The Magic, Mystery And New Friendships Made At Stone Doll Holler

As I continued visiting this area, I began noticing that I was capturing images of various, seemingly curious observers on my videos and photos. Seeing new individuals almost every time I visit there. I will share a few of them in this chapter with you.

On May 16, 2022, I thought I would try something to see if it would get any results. I asked for permission to use my camera, as always out of respect. After all, you wouldn't want someone to come into your home and start taking photos of you, would you?

I told them that if they wouldn't mind letting me see them, I would love it. I also said "if you don't want me to see you, just keep yourselves hidden." Then I snapped a few photos. Later that night, looking through the photos, I zoomed in on each one to see if I could spot anything.

To my surprise I saw 3 individuals in one photo, all fairly close to one another. Zooming in, I screenshot the photo a few times to get a closer look.

Very blurry because of being zoomed in so much but I circled the 3 beings I saw.

Zoomed in even closer. He appears to be smiling! I call him Mr. Smiley.

Obvious one on the left & "something" peeking thru the bushes right side. You can only see its eyes and chin.

It appears to be "dogman" like.

Small beady eyes and dark hair on its face.

Now for the little gnome looking being on the far left of first photo. He has fat little cheeks!

Eyes dotted by me for reference.

I showed a friend these photos. She has been interacting with and is familiar with many different cryptids for more than 65 years. She said the little gnome looking being is what people call the "Little People of the Forest". And the one I call Mr. Smiley was called a Stone Man. I'm not sure what the other one is. Its appearance looks a bit "werewolfish". There are many other beings and cryptid creatures we know nothing about out there besides Bigfoot. We will take a look at a few of them in this chapter.

I have also encountered what I later learned was called a Cat Person. Here is an incredible screenshot from a video I was taking at this location.

Notice the smiling face on the right side and the Cat being on the left. Also, a peeker above!

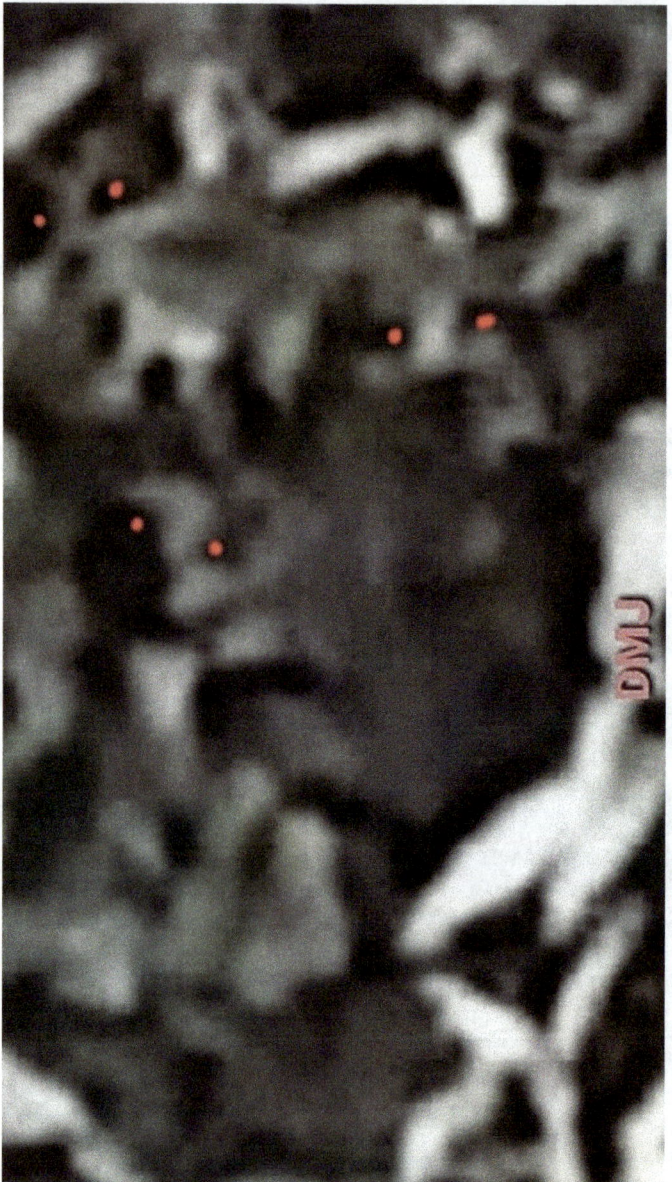

Eyes dotted by me

The Cat Person appears to have a very long neck and also appears to have a smile on its face. I printed this and framed it. As I was doing so, I had the photo turned on its side. Take a look at what else I found!

I know it is blurry, but I see what looks like a bigfoot with his head tilted back.

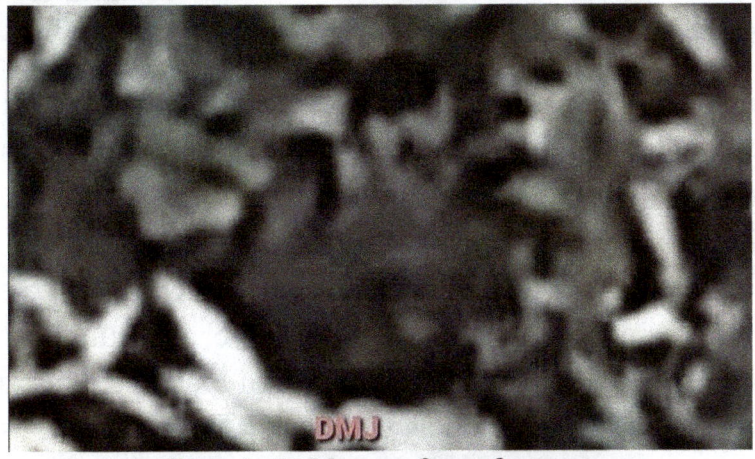

Eyes dotted by me for reference.

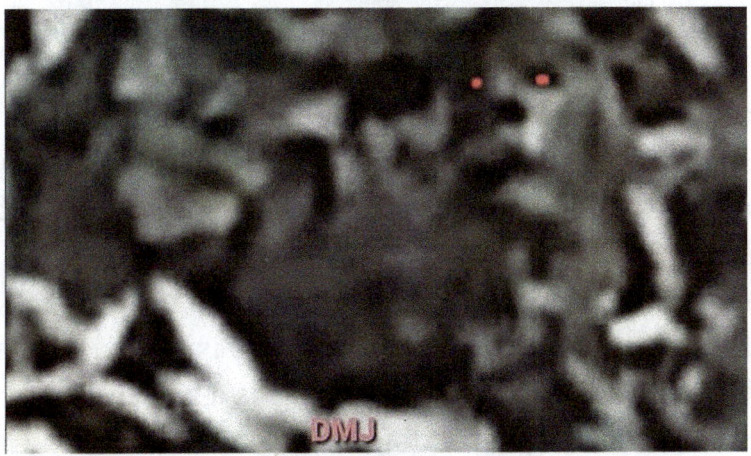

They never cease to amaze me how they can blend in with their surroundings. It has taken me many years to be able to spot them on the videos. I know I still pass right by many of them, not noticing them, but am getting better at it. I learned some things to look for, so I know where to stop and take a screenshot from the video. If I see a blurry spot, I always take a closer look. They can somehow make their presence appear as a "blur" on your camera. If it is a photo, always look for eyes and go from there. You will be surprised at the detail you will see at times. An entire face and sometimes the body too, just by looking for the eyes.

One of my favorites, which by the way I also have had as a lock screen on my phone for years, is this gentle giant that I am about to show you. I had established one (of many) gifting spots at this location, and would hang things in the tree for them there. I purchased a little metal Christmas mailbox from the dollar store, and hung it from some string. I would fill it full of crackers, nuts, and animal cookies for them as well as various other things at different times. Then I would shut the door on the mailbox. In this way, I would know if they had been there to get the goodies out of the box. They would normally take the food out of the box then politely shut the door back on it once it was emptied. On this occasion, I had Eric filming me because my hands were full, and wanted to document what we were doing. Later, upon replaying the video, I saw her. She has somehow communicated mentally to me that she is a female. I can't explain how, but she has. Next page is a screenshot from the video showing me adding things to the mailbox. Can you see her?

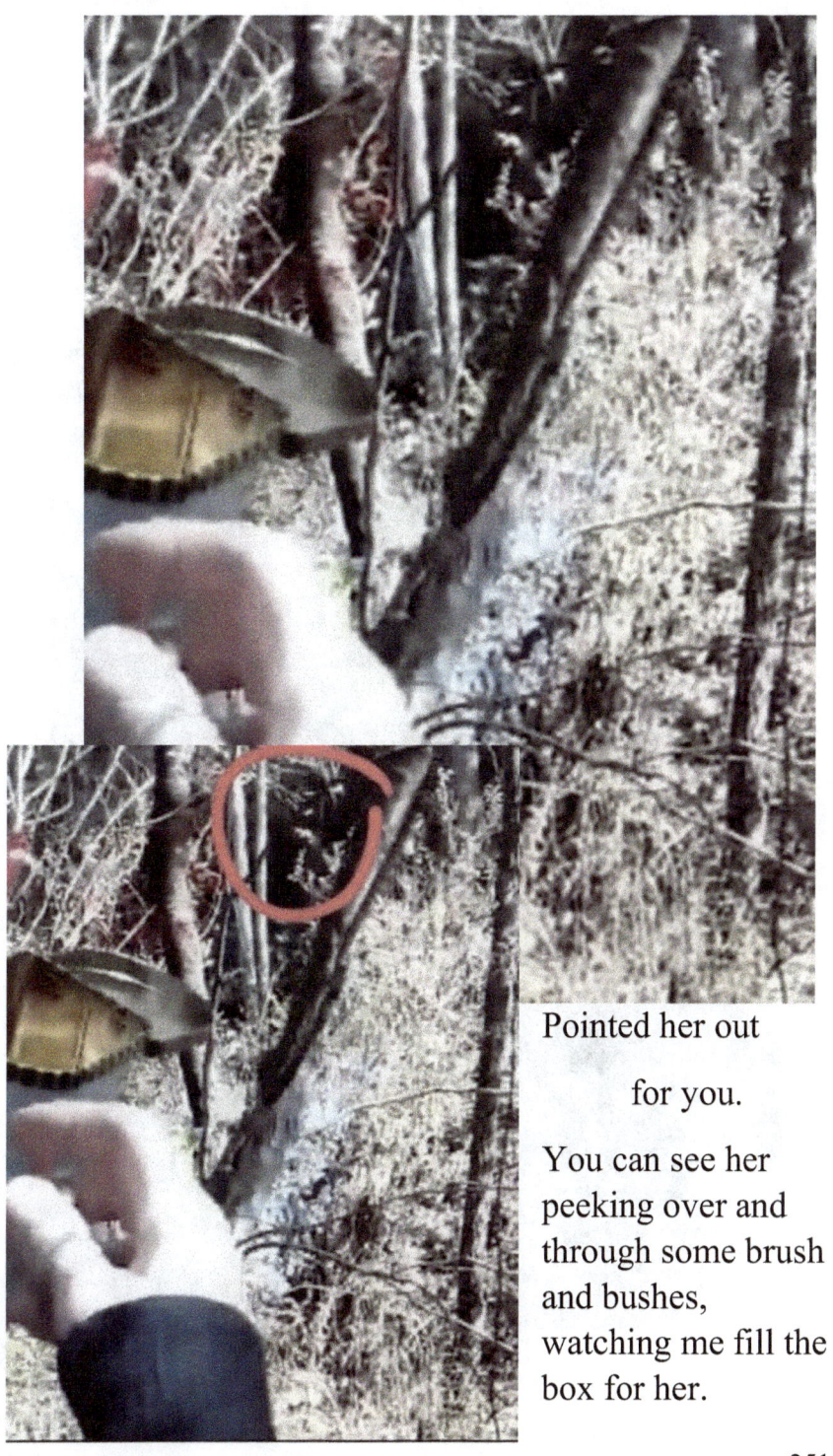

Pointed her out for you.

You can see her peeking over and through some brush and bushes, watching me fill the box for her.

Now for a closer look.

I have zoomed in a lot & changed the color to

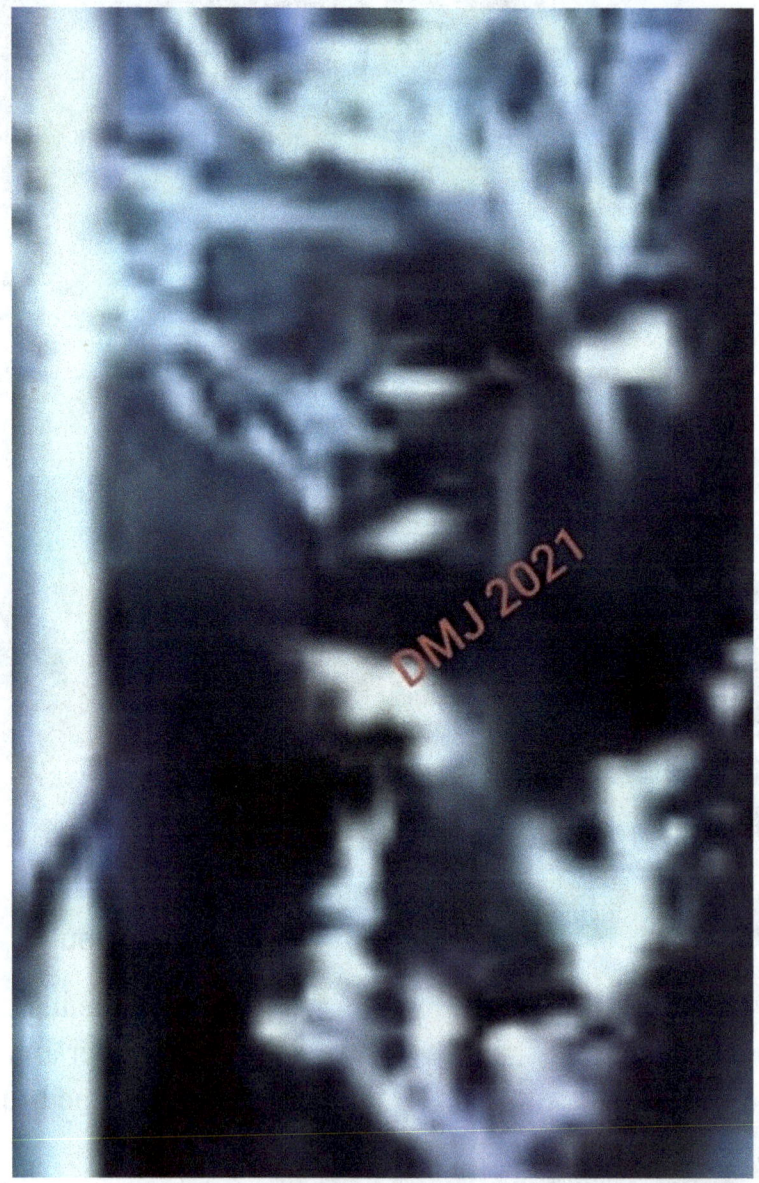

enhance it a bit. See her eyes? Dotted by me next for reference.

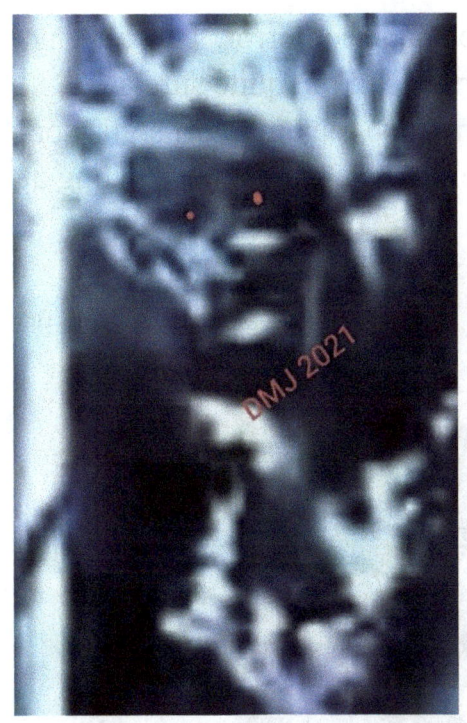

I see she has whites in her eyes. Not as some people say that their eyes are all black. I have this photo also framed and hanging on my wall of memories at home. I absolutely love her gentle eyes!

Now for another encounter that wasn't so gentle or nice. On January 4, 2022, I was at Stone Doll Holler. This was during a time when my Forest Friends had been absent for a couple of months. I do not know where they were, but it was such a sad time. During the time they were away, there was an odd, "off" feeling there. It just wasn't normal, and I got very bad vibes whenever I visited.

I was walking around and heard a low growling right behind me. And I mean I could feel the breath! Every hair on my body stood at attention and chills immediately hit me. Spinning around, I saw absolutely nothing. I immediately headed to the truck and started filming toward the area where it occured. I saw a juvenile dogman peeking around a cedar tree, through the limbs at me. I will admit, it was terrifying. I had never visually seen a dogman before, although I had a run in with one which I will devote an entire chapter to. It was not a pleasant experience. Panic and sheer terror. These beings seem to exude fear and terror. I'm not quite sure as to why. Do they mean us harm? Do they give off some sort of energy that we can "feel"? Was this being growling at me to let me know he was there, or did he mean me harm? I suppose if he meant me harm, He could have easily done whatever he wanted to with me. Here is a screenshot from the video I was taking at the time.

Juvenile dogman peeking around the cedar tree at me.

Next page, eyes dotted by me for reference.

Not long after this experience, maybe a week or two afterwards, in this same area, Eric saw what he described as a werewolf standing in the tree line watching us. It was only about 30 feet from where we were standing. I could not see it even though I looked intently in the direction he said it was standing. He said it was solid black and approximately 7 feet tall. It just stood there motionless. Then he said it simply just disappeared. He completely lost sight of it. I suppose maybe it wanted Eric to see it and it revealed itself to him. I just didn't see it. But I believe him. If you know Eric, he is not one to fabricate stories. As a matter of fact, sometimes he will not even share things with me for quite some time because he feels they are too far "out there". So, I know that he did see something.

I was never so happy when the Forest People finally returned and "cleaned house." Everything went back to normal, and the vibes were good again. We never had another bad experience there.

Speaking of dogman, I captured another photo of one with a Forest Person. This happened in August of 2022, just a few months after the prior incident spoken of. We were close to the same area. I was standing in an open area and looking at the water. I always look close by the water for tracks because sometimes I find them in the wet sand and dirt. Standing there, I heard a loud, gravely cough or huff behind me coming from the tree line. So, I took out my phone and snapped a few photos. A few days later I looked closer at the photos. Zooming in, lo and behold, I saw a Bigfoot peeking around a tree and a dogman peeking around another tree right beside him. Here is the original photo. I marked where they are. I

<u>Original photo. Arrows pointing to their location.</u>

know it's impossible to see them here. Zooming in closer, this is what I saw.

<u>Forest Person on the left and dogman on the right.</u>

Now dotting the eyes for reference just in case you still do not see them.

I was thrilled to see them there.

But then a puzzling thought. If the Forest People took over the area and ran the dogman beings away just months prior, why would these two be here together? Do they run together? Are they friendly with each other? I suppose, maybe just as we humans get along with certain people and don't necessarily get along with other people, maybe they do the same thing. And we all have our own personalities that draw us to certain people and not to others. There are good and bad in every species.

Now as if this was not incredible enough, I posted these photos on my Facebook page. And someone pointed out that there was something else in this same photo. When they showed this to me, I was in shock.

Close by these 2 beings was another being. One of which I have never encountered and

truly thought was only in myth and legend. He pointed out there was a fairy there. I had to really look hard to see that one. But when I spotted her, I was blown away. You can obviously see it's a female. She has her arm on the right side raised up in the air. Her other arm is down and bent at the elbow. Appears to be her wing on the left side too. Her legs are together and bent at the knees. You can even see her feet.

<u>A closer view of the fairy</u>.

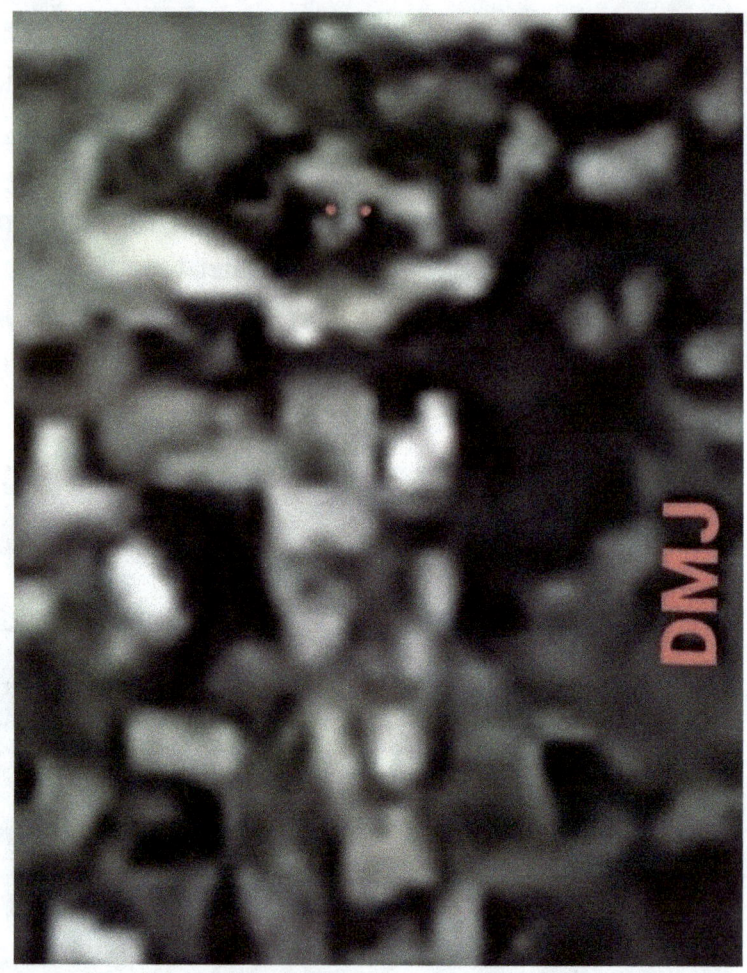

Why was this fairy there with these other 2 beings? She must have wanted us to see her. I don't believe it's any accident when you are shown these things, I believe it's their choice whether you see them or not. **<u>Eyes dotted for reference here.</u>**

There are so many different beings out there that we don't know about. Some we have never heard of and some we only believed were myths. I will include a few photos and screenshots of some different individuals we have encountered here at Stone Doll Holler. I do not know what they are all called. There are many of them and they all have different characteristics. I will just share the images here. They were all captured on my videos and photos.

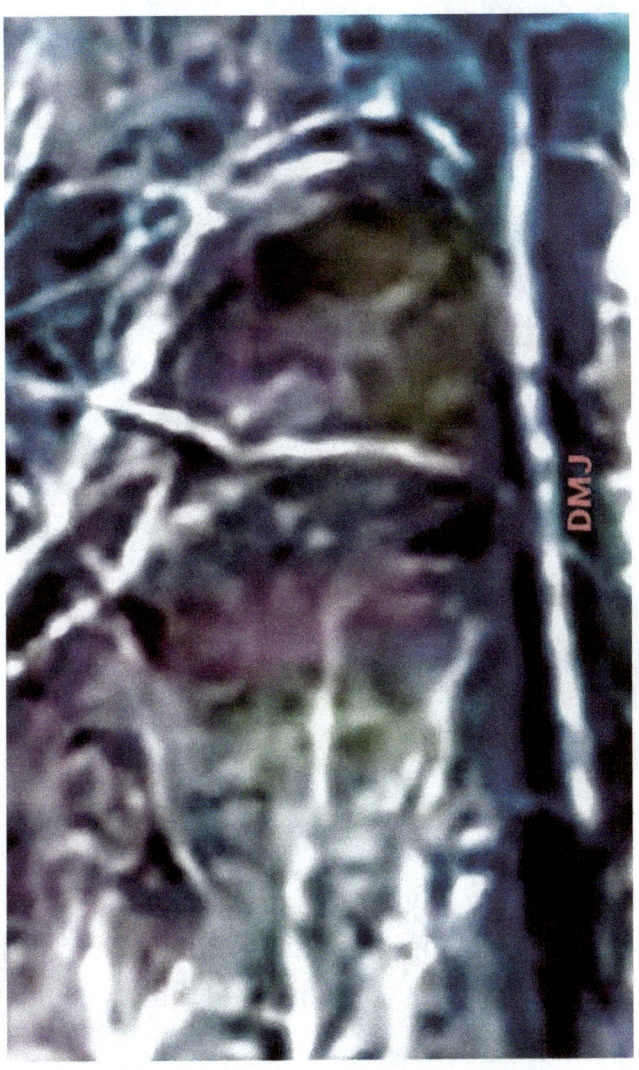

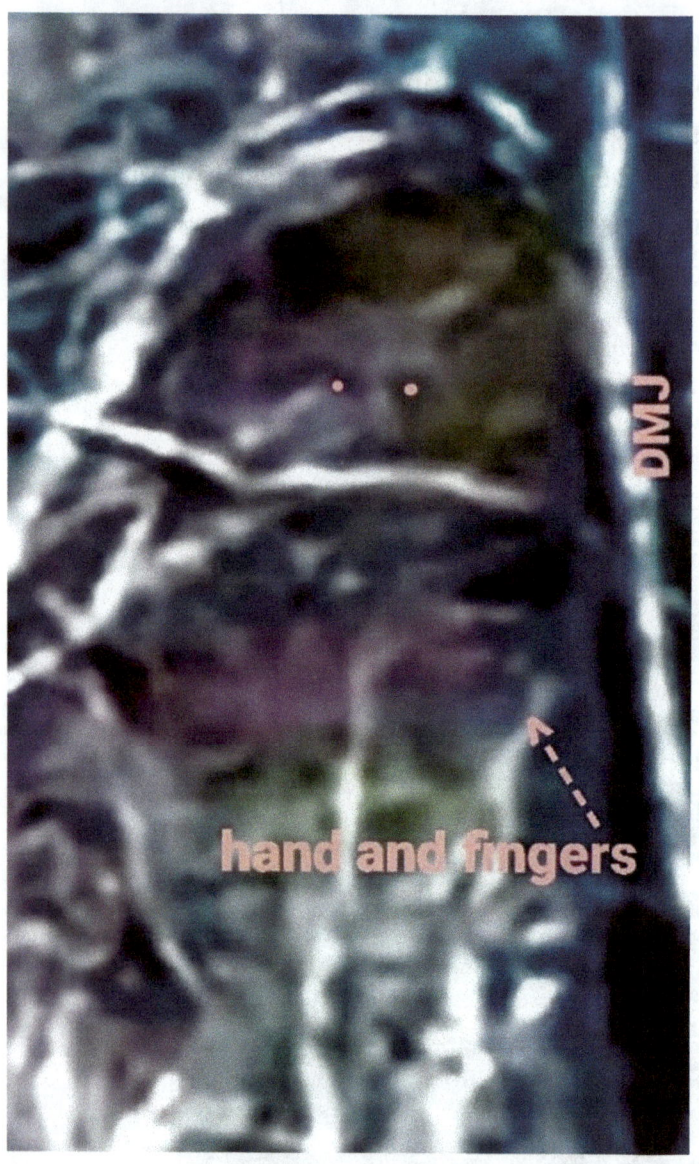

It appears this one may have horns or ears on top of its head. Here is another being that I accidentally captured on a video. There is always someone watching when we visit here.

This one has somewhat of a "rat" appearance. But this was no rat. I spotted this guy on a video I took, and he was at least 60 feet away. And he was BIG.

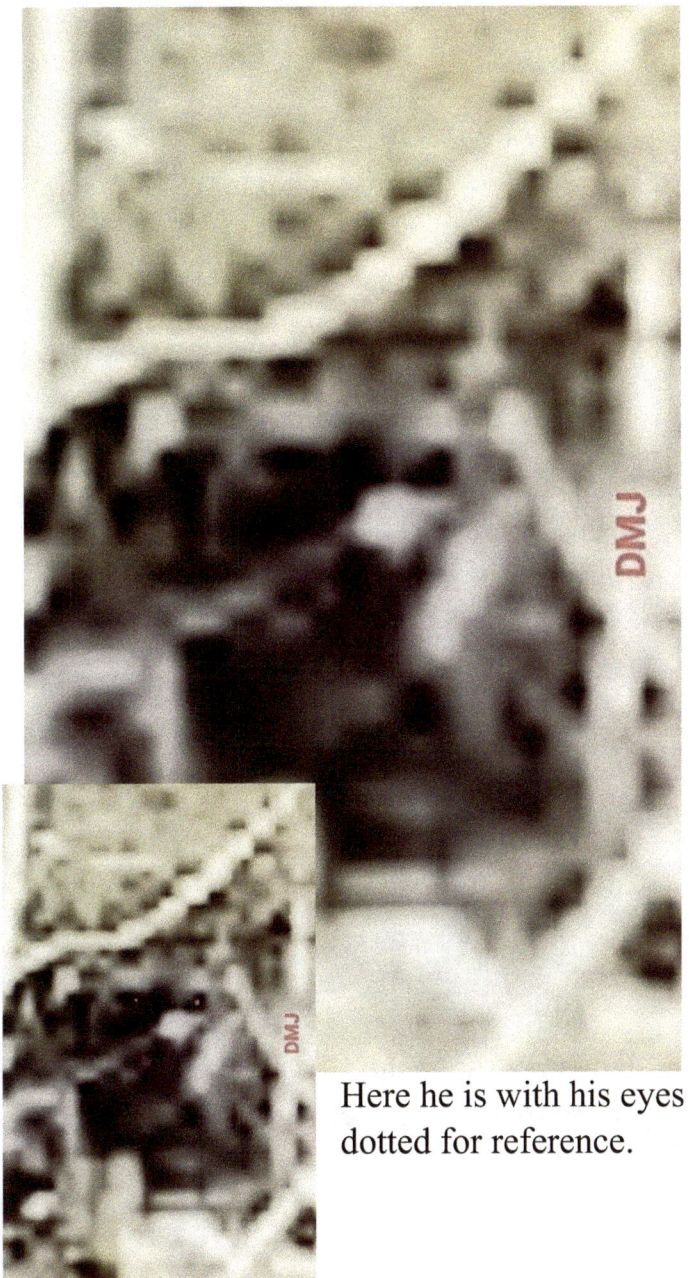

Here he is with his eyes dotted for reference.

Next is a screenshot from a video I took when my

granddaughter Aubree and I were visiting one of the gifting trees there. Let's get a closer look.

Let's get closer.

Eyes dotted by me for reference. He appears to be smiling!

Even though it is pixelated from all of the zooming in and screenshotting it multiple times, you can see its face. It was standing in a ditch peeking over the embankment at us.

They seem to be attracted to Aubree. I believe because she is an innocent child and they like people with the demeanor of a child. Not spoiled by the world. They have not been indoctrinated with what is possible and what is not. Their minds are open to possibilities most adults consider impossible.

I myself have known from the very beginning (as I told you about in Chapter one) that nothing is impossible. I knew this before even being born. My mind is as wide open as it possibly can be. I believe this is why the Forest People and other beings are attracted to me as well. They know I can "see", and they show themselves when they want me to see them. And I'm grateful that they do.

Here is another screenshot from a video I took there. Posting this video to my Facebook page, a friend spotted this being, that I will show you next, watching from under the brush. He converted it to black and white. I took the screenshot he sent me, zoomed in and cropped

out the face and put the two photos side by side. This is to show how they can be mere feet away from you and you will not even be aware of their presence. This being has such a human face. Yet not human at all.

Eyes dotted by me for reference in the second photo. This curious being appears to be lying on the ground peeking from behind all the tall brush and bushes.

Now I have another story to share about Stone Doll Holler. First, I will share a little bit more about the place with you.

This is a very remote area in the middle of complete wilderness. It is down a one lane gravel (well, not really gravel…just rock) road down the side of a mountain. When you are headed down there, it seems you are entering into an entirely different world. Seriously. At the bottom is a holler with a small opening that is clear. It's about 3 miles down to the bottom on this rocky road. There are no houses for many, many miles. I also have to drive around 10 more miles out into the country to even get to this rocky road. There is one way in and one way out. When you get down to the bottom, you feel sort of "trapped". Any living being in the entire area already knows you are coming down there before you even get there. You have to creep down this mountain as the road is very rough and rocky. The only way out after arriving at the bottom is to turn around and creep back up the mountain on the road or climb up the side of a huge bluff. And I'm not much of a mountain goat! Once you are there, you are there, and you can feel the eyes on you. Piercing right through you. You are being closely observed. There is a small creek running through there that has a nice cold spring where we find a lot of footprints and stick glyphs. We leave gifts here and are gifted back various things.

We visited here on September 23, 2020. On this particular day, we were already startled because we had found what appeared to be pools of blood by the water and footprints all around. Now, as we walk around surveying the area, we start hearing loud pops and trees snapping in different directions and what sounded like vocals off in the distance.

Then, as we approach the tree line and brush, we hear growling. Every time we got near the tall brush in front of the tree line, the growling started again. It was a very low-pitched growl. One that made you question for sure if it WAS a growl. But it was definitely a growl. One we could "feel" more than hear. I can't explain it any better than that. We "felt" the growl. It went right through us.

Of course, as is my usual, I was taking a video at the time. This video is where I took the following screenshots from. I watched as Eric made his way forward towards the brush and tree line. We heard and "felt" the growl. He immediately turned and began to come back toward me. But he is a curious type and wanted to know what was growling at him. So, he went back once again toward the tree line. Again, the growling

started. I pleaded with him to come back and get in the truck and get away from there. He FINALLY did and I was so relieved. The pools of blood we had seen earlier really spooked me. After returning home, I watched the video, and spotted a big, dark shape in the background. I paused the video. That is the screenshot I took.

Here I circled what I found when zooming in.

Let's look closer. Our suspect is hiding back there between 2 trees.

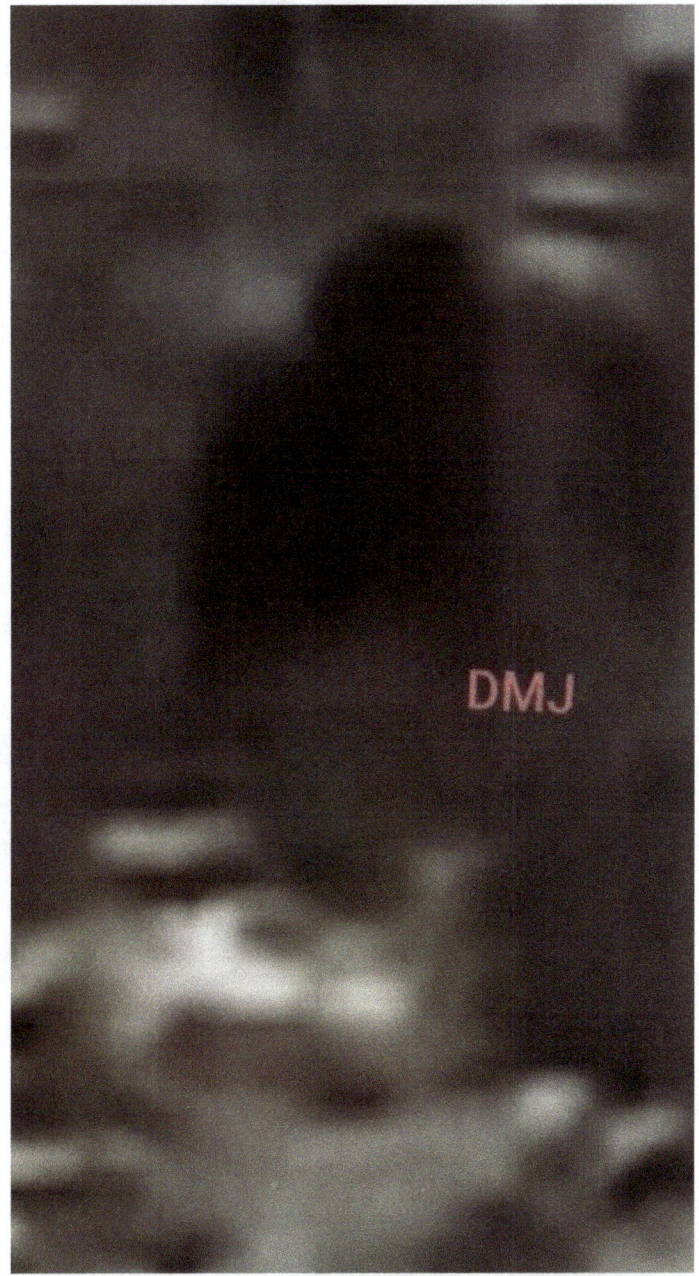

Why is the suspect growling? Let's look closer!

Three babies here! One's head is cocked to the side.

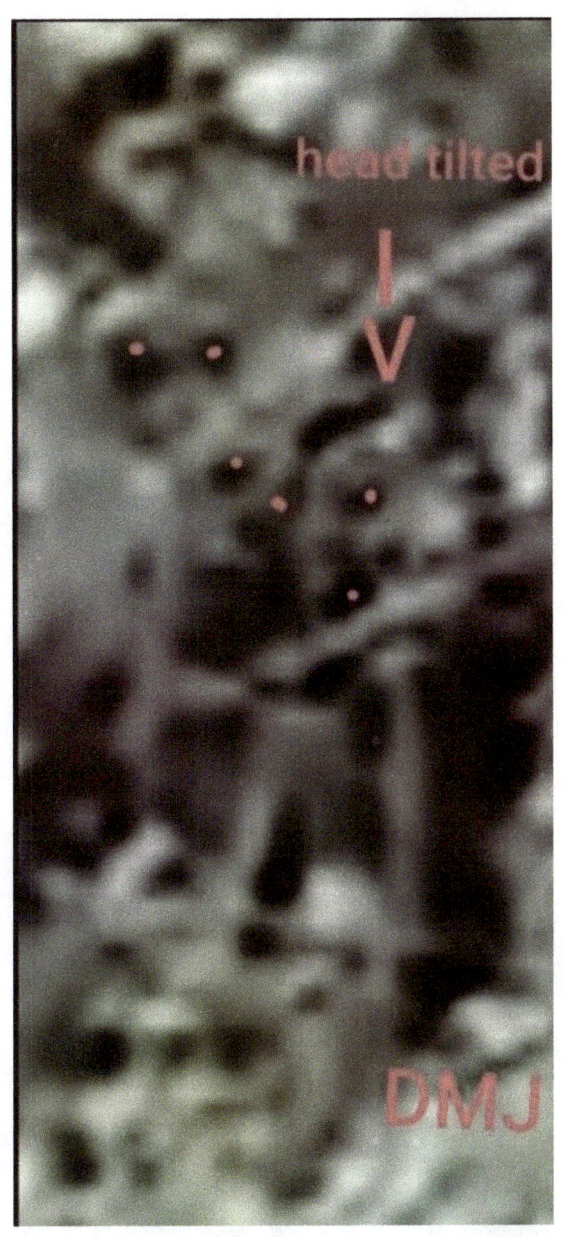

Eyes dotted by me for reference.

They are so cute! The babies were hiding in the brush and whoever was in the tree line was protecting them. Hence, every time Eric got close, he or she began growling. Pure instinct. Protect the young from any possible danger. I apologized to them, and we left them in peace.

Chapter 23
The Warning On Terror Mountain

I have somewhat to say. It boggles my mind what our bigfoot friends are able to do. This may sound like a bunch of nonsense to some, but I swear this is the absolute truth.

On August 15, 2019, Eric received in the mail a bigfoot necklace I had ordered for him. He was so proud of it and never took it off.

There is no need to expound or exaggerate on any of these details. I am just laying out the facts and the "strangeness" to you all. On Wednesday, March 03, 2021, we decided to take a hike on a new trail we had discovered from an earlier hike but were too tired to continue on that particular day. We also decided that since we didn't know how far this trail went or how long we would be out there, we would stop and buy a backpack cooler and some food and drinks. As we entered the store to purchase these things, Eric's Bigfoot necklace pendant fell onto the floor. We just figured his chain had broken or the bail holding the pendant to the chain had opened a bit. To our disbelief, his chain was intact and still clasped around his neck and the bail was completely closed tight on the pendant. Somehow the closed bail passed through a solid chain. We investigated by intently looking at the pendant and found no reason whatsoever why it had fallen off of the chain. I had an eerie feeling that something was wrong, but I shrugged it off and continued shopping and gathering our food and drinks before heading to the trail.

That day, for no apparent reason, I was feeling uneasy about the whole situation. I could not pinpoint any specific reason for this fearful feeling. I just shrugged it off and continued the journey to the newfound trail and all the excitement that lay ahead, anticipating what new things we would discover.

This trail is approximately 15 miles into the forest as you travel down a rough gravel road. It is very secluded with thick massive trees all around. As we approached the area, the uneasiness got stronger and stronger. We had to park at the top of a very tall bluff. As I exited the vehicle, I began having horrible thoughts. The first thing I said was "I hope bigfoot doesn't push the truck off of this bluff!" As we descended down the mountain, I heard one loud very odd sounding "crow" call, then it went completely silent. I kept thinking unnatural thoughts. I am normally very at home in the woods, but this day, I was definitely not at all. I began to tell Eric "I hope we don't run into a Momma bear with cubs" When have I ever feared the woods like this?

We reached the bottom of the mountain beside the water and were unable to cross because the water was too high. I had this ominous feeling as tho something was watching and following us. I heard leaves crunching off to our side about 50 feet away. Since we were unable to cross the water, we turned around and started back up the mountain. There was another smaller trail that veered off to the left. There was a large fallen tree blocking that path and we had to go around it to get on that trail. Why was that tree blocking this small path? This trail was different. It was much narrower and felt even more disturbing to me. I walked about 100 feet into this area and felt an urgency to turn around and go back. To quickly LEAVE this area. I told Eric I was sorry, but I was not feeling good at all about what we were doing. He then finally admitted that he too was feeling dread and doom. We turned around and made our way back up the mountain to the truck. It seemed like an eternity to achieve this task. I felt such a sense of relief as we entered the safety of our vehicle and headed back down the mountain.

We stopped at the bottom of the mountain before going through a closed gate. Eric had a call for nature and went off out of sight to relieve himself. As he stood there a rabbit came bounding towards him. That was very unusual. At this same time, I was standing beside the truck. I heard one single, very loud crow call. Then something began walking down the wooded mountain behind me. This thing was walking on two legs, taking bipedal steps, and sounded like it was unnaturally large as it moved through the trees and brush. Leaves were crunching and sticks were breaking. I yelled at Eric to warn him of this. At that very moment, a rock was thrown at one of the abandoned farmhouse buildings. We decided we better get out of there! No wonder that rabbit ran towards Eric. Eric was substantially less threating to it than whatever was lurking in the woods!

We decided to head out of there by traveling further down this same road in the same direction. It is a bit closer to get out if you don't go back the way you come in. It goes all the way from one area to another. As we went on down the road, I too felt the call of nature. We stopped again about a quarter of a mile down the road. As I went over behind a big rock to relieve myself, I again heard one single loud crow call. Then, "CRUNCH, CRUNCH!" and sticks being broken. It was the same bipedal walking I heard down the road. How did this thing travel through the woods a quarter of a mile so fast on foot? It was following us and stalking us! I ran back to the truck and yelled "It's following us!!" We headed a bit farther down the road and could not cross the high water. We had to turn around and go back the way we had come from. Oh no! I didn't know what was stalking us, but I certainly did not want to run into it. We managed to turn around and headed out of there as fast as we could. Then as we drove farther and farther for what seemed like an eternity, I realized "I don't recognize where I'm at." This area is one I have frequented for the last 35+ years and I normally know every bit of the surroundings. I was very confused and didn't see anything that I recognized whatsoever. Finally, as we went farther down the road, I saw something that I did recognize. What a sense of relief I had at that moment. But why was I lost in an area I knew so well?

We made our way home at last and talked about what all had happened. Eric disclosed to me that all along he was having a feeling of dread too and that he felt we shouldn't be going to the area, but he shrugged it off just as I did thinking it would ruin our fun if it was mentioned. Then we realized that the bigfoot pendant of his necklace that fell off with no apparent cause (impossible) was possibly a warning to not go to that trail. Our Friends must have been warning us to stay away from that area. That there was something with bad intentions lurking in those woods that day. We just didn't understand their message at the time. Eric rarely removed his necklace for quite some time after that. It was our connection to communicate with our Forest Friends.

Necklace as it was on closed bail

Bail was completely closed. The bail had passed through a solid chain and hit the floor while we were shopping.

The pendant falling off the unbroken chain happened once again. It was March 12, 2021. It was Eric's birthday. We were sitting at my mother's house when it simply fell in his lap with the bail still on the pendant. My mother also witnessed this strange occurrence on that day. It is my belief that they were telling him "Happy Birthday my human brother!"

Once again, on May 24th, 2021, more strangeness. Instead of the closed bail coming off of the chain, the pendant fell off of the closed bail! The bail was tightly clasped together and there was no way this could naturally happen.

Necklace after the pendant fell off of the bail.

The last time it happened, it "broke the camel's back". This was on June 4, 2021. We had taken the bail off of the necklace and added a small split ring on the pendant so it would virtually be impossible for the pendant to fall off. It had to be twisted around the metal piece as you would a key on a keyring to get it on and off. He put the necklace back on. After wearing it for about 30 minutes, as we sat at the kitchen table, the ring that holds the clasp to the back of the necklace came apart and the entire necklace fell onto the table right in front of

Split ring we added "guaranteeing" the pendant could not fall off.

us. But once again, the links were closed tightly. It was as if the 2 solid links passed right through each other. He never put that necklace on again. He determined that he had had ENOUGH!

Necklace after it fell onto the table.

Chapter 24

Why Are They Always Blurry?

Why are they ALWAYS blurry? How many times have I been asked that question. It gets monotonous repeating myself over and over trying to explain it every single time. It is a researchers' nightmare trying to explain to people who, by the way, will most likely never believe it no matter what you say. Most of the time, they have ill intentions and are just asking this question to make fun of anyone who has actually had an encounter or has captured a photo or video of a bigfoot.

Once in a while, someone will ask this who truly wants to learn. This chapter is for those people. For those who may have trouble grasping the bigfoots seemingly impossible abilities but truly want to learn more about them. Something it has taken me quite a while to come to grips with. I will try my best to explain these things in the same way that it finally made sense to me. This is from my own personal experience.

It's not an easy task, by any means, to comprehend all of this until you start digging deeper into scientific facts such as vibrational frequencies.

Everything in the universe, down to a speck of dust, has a vibrational frequency. That is a scientific fact. We all vibrate on different frequencies. The Sasquatch People seem to have a higher vibrational frequency than you and I. They also seem to have the ability to CONTROL their vibrational frequency.

Think of the movie "Predator". They can and do appear in this way. I personally have seen them in this form. I have also witnessed one simply "vanish" in front of me. It did not actually vanish. It simply changed form by controlling its vibration so that my eyes were unable to see it.

Now, back to the blurriness. Add the fact that our cameras can "see" things that we physically do not see at the time, such as orbs, for example. The camera can pick up on them. Also, add the fact that most people are utilizing a phone camera to take a video or photo of anything they may come across because most of us have access to a phone most of the time.

In the case of videos, we are zooming in, and the video, of course, is also moving. Zooming in pixelates the images on the camera. Now, pause that moving video and take a screenshot. Then zoom in even further to "investigate" a suspicious image that you see. That pixelates and distorts the image even more. This happens even if you are examining a photograph you took while standing completely still. It gets very pixelated as you zoom in on a specific area of the picture.

You will never get a "clear" image of a sasquatch unless they WANT you to see them. They can and do control this. I have seen them in "solid, physical" form (for lack of a better term) but they are in control of how you see them and what you actually see. They are, in fact, solid physical beings but can control their ability to pass through solid walls by changing their vibrational frequency if they choose to do so. We would have this ability as well if we learned to control our vibrational frequency. Some say we did at one time also have this ability but have just lost it somewhere along the way. Back to the closed mind.

I hope this will help you to understand their abilities and understand why most photos are blurry. And how they can do things that seem like an impossible task such as walking right into a tree and passing through it. Or seeming to vanish right in front of you. They are not actually vanishing. They do this by controlling their vibrational frequency.

I'm no scientist, but I have experienced this, and the theory explains a lot to me and helps me to understand more about these remarkable People.

Chapter 25
Close to Home

This chapter is dedicated to the beings who live around my property and my home. It seems that once you become aware of the bigfoot's existence, they are drawn to you. If you have good intentions towards them, they are eager to teach you more. It is as though you are a lighthouse on a very dark night and when they see you, they draw near, howbeit most subtly most of the time. And subsequently, once you are drawn to them, you begin to notice every evidence of their existence all around you. Things you never noticed before. It is a mutual attraction.

I have an array of individuals who live around me. My backyard is always an exhilarating place for me to visit. Very rarely does it disappoint. I visit the woods behind the house quite frequently when the weather allows. When my granddaughters Aubree and Michelle are with me, it seems to provoke even more communication from our Forest Friends. They seem to really love children. They will "Whoop", clack rocks and make all sorts of noises when my grandchildren are here.

There is a spot where we like to go and sit next to the woods behind the house. This is our special spot and I believe the bigfoot know why we are there. At times, I go up there and sit and sing to my Friends who are hiding in those woods but are drawing near to see me and to listen to me. One day, I was sitting there singing "This Is My Fathers World". It is a song I love, and we sing in church occasionally. After singing it to them a couple of times, I asked them if they would allow me to take a picture of them. I told them that if they would allow me to see them, I would love it. But if they chose to remain hidden, I would understand. Then I took a few photos. Later that day, I looked through the photos, zooming in on every bit of the pictures to see if I spotted any of my Friends in them. I was so happy to find a warmhearted, contented, pleased face looking back at me! Here on the left is a close up of one of them. Can you see the face? Let's zoom in closer….

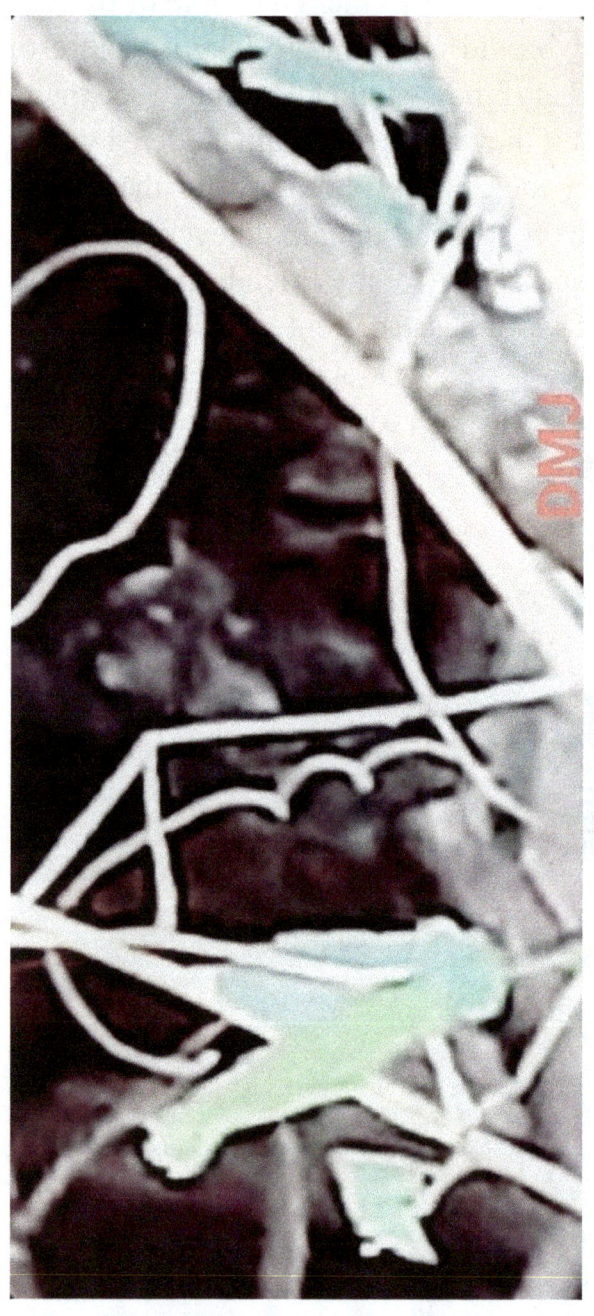

You can see on the right side of the photo, there is a branch concealing one of its eyes. They almost always reveal "just enough" of themselves, so that I know they are there. Next I dotted the eyes for reference:

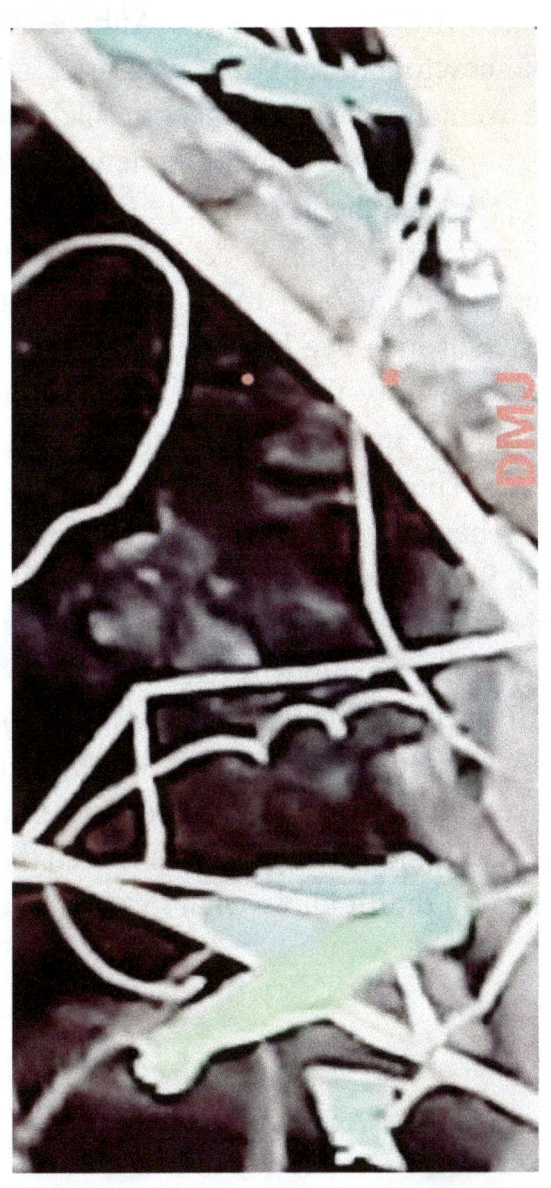

I can see a small, slanted eye on the left side, an ear on the same side, a wide flat nose, a wide mouth, and a large chin. They wanted to let me know that they were listening to me singing. I believe I captured this photo of them as a thank you.

Another time, my granddaughter Aubree and I were exploring a newfound trail that ventured off into the woods. We went further back than we had ever been. It was very exciting to find something new to explore back there! As we traveled the new trail, I took a video. I posted the video for my friends on Facebook to see. One of my friends saw something and took a screenshot from the video. To my surprise, we had walked right by two baby bigfoot and never saw them while we were there. There was something else I noticed about this screenshot that she had sent to me. The older baby was holding what appeared to be a teddy bear. About six months earlier, I had given my little dog Shorty a teddy bear toy. He didn't care much about it. He isn't much of one to play with toys, but I wanted to get it for him anyway to snuggle with in his bed. He had left it lying on the porch. Then one day it mysteriously disappeared. I didn't know where it had gone. I looked all around the porch and even checked to see if it had fallen off of the porch. I checked the yard, and it was not there. I didn't know what to make of it and soon forgot about it. But there it was in that screenshot. The baby bigfoot was holding it!

Two baby bigfoots. The older one is holding the smaller baby bigfoot. Also, notice how his ears stick out! Cuteness overload!

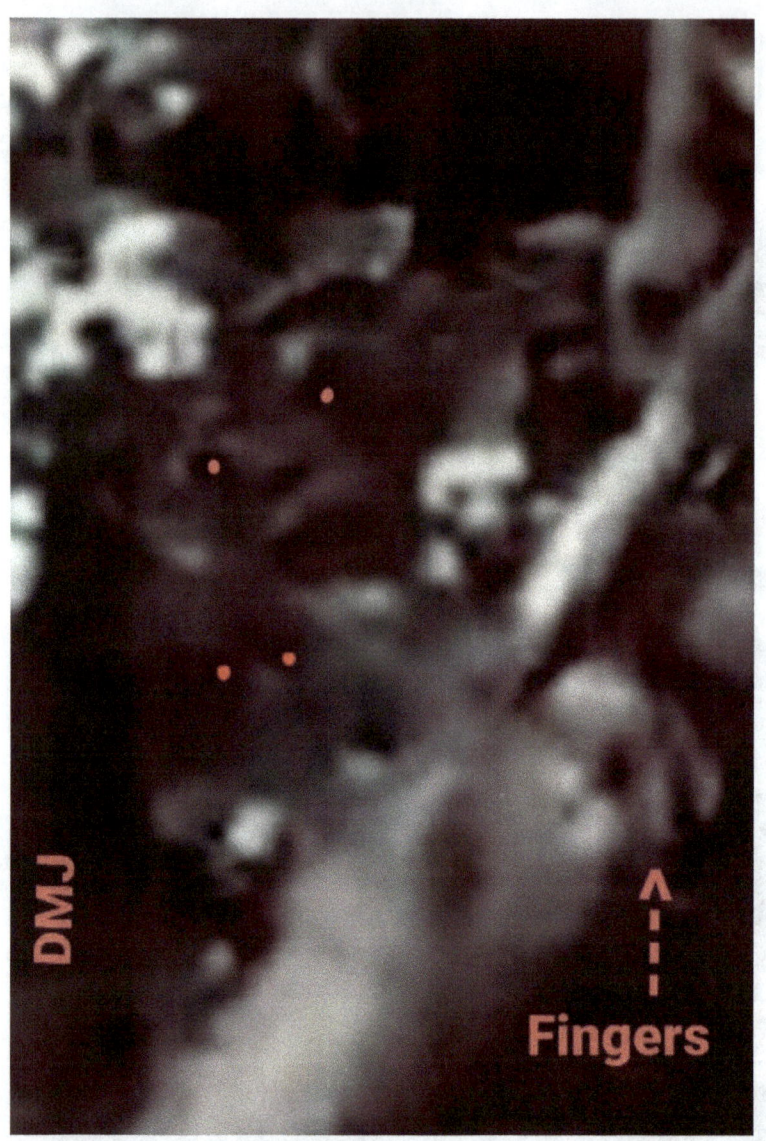

Here I have dotted the eyes for reference. Look to the right of the top one's face. You will see the white teddy bear toy!

But it didn't end there. We walked that trail on Friday. On Monday morning, I began experiencing a lot of odd noises in the house. I would occasionally hear a big bang on the wall right beside me. I would hear loud exhales of breath in the next room. My bedroom door opened, and I heard footsteps. All sorts of strange noises. I got upset thinking I had a new spirit or ghost who was "moving in". I tried to think of anything I may have purchased at a flea market etc. that may have had an attachment to it. As I explained in Chapter 12, this had happened to me before. I loudly exclaimed "You are not welcome here! You have to go. In the name of Jesus Christ, I command you to get out of my house!" To my dismay, that did not seem to work. The activity continued for 3 days. Then on the fourth day as I woke up, I went into the bathroom. In this bathroom I have a dark burgundy carpet. Because it is a solid dark color, it shows everything that lands on it. There beside the tub was an obvious footprint. It was white. My feet nor any of my grandchildren's feet are this small. Aubree can wear my shoes. And no one had been to my house with any children. I looked closely at it, and I saw 5 toes and a heel. Next is a photo I took of it:

You can clearly see a footprint on the rug.

There is no way that came from a person in my house. I do not know anyone with a foot that small and Aubree was the only one who had been in my house. How can this be? Then it dawned on me. The baby bigfoot we walked by 5 days ago on the trail. It must have followed Aubree and I home. I was overcome with guilt. I felt so bad for yelling at this baby to get out of my house and that it was not welcome. The noises stopped after I found this print. I hope he or she knows I mistook them for a ghost. I don't want them upset with me. I suppose they must know that we are not as smart as they are, and we misunderstand things that we cannot explain. I hope the baby found its way home.

On another occasion, my daughter Amber and my granddaughter Aubree were visiting me. This was in August of 2022. We walked up in the back yard to see if we could see anything. There are many big trees up there and occasionally we find stick structures and stick glyphs up there as well as other things. As we walked, I found a blue jay feather. I had been finding random blue jay feathers almost every day at that point and time. I had already acquired about 5 or 6 of them in the days prior to this. At the same exact time that I picked up the blue jay feather, Aubree exclaimed "I found a big crow feather!". We were bragging about being gifted with these things. Amber said, "I wish I could find something." I looked at where she was, and she looked down, never moving from that spot, nor taking a step. There sitting on the ground at her feet was a big pinecone. There are no pine trees anywhere around there.

Our feathers and Amber's big pinecone

She was gifted as well as us! How do they do this? Maybe it's a coincidence. But as I said, I don't really put stock in "coincidences".

After this happened, Amber said she felt the need to take a photo towards the tree line. She does not normally take photos randomly as I do of the woods. Although I am a researcher and I go out doing that sort of thing, she is not really into it. But that day she said she felt compelled to take a photo. Here it is:

Let's look closer:

Do you see the two faces in there? They were right there watching us. The one at the top appears to have an orb or a white spot right between its eyes. What a great capture.

At times, I randomly take pictures of this same tree line. As I said, I have a special place up there that I sit and talk to my Friends. There was another occasion when I was there talking with them, and I asked if I could take some photos. I said I would love to see them if they didn't mind. I do this occasionally because it helps me to know in my heart that they are there. That I am not just up there talking to myself. On this day I took several pictures.

As I have previously mentioned in Chapter 18, we became acquainted with Urijah's little brother Timothy. He loves to be recognized and he occasionally draws self-portraits of himself on the ground as I showed in that same chapter. I recognize him now when I see him. I have pictures of him with Urijah in the woods watching me as I walked down to leave gifts for them.

The place where they live is about 15 to 20 miles from my house. That is my research areas that I named Dead Man's Mountain and Footprint Alley. That is their home.

One day I took pictures of the tree line behind my house as I stated before. I look through the pictures I take carefully. I zoom in to see if I see anyone in there because as you know, they are camouflage experts. On this particular day, I captured an individual that looked very familiar. It looked like Timothy.

Here is a portion of that photo, zoomed in & cropped. If you look in the center, you will see his face. He has his hand up to his mouth area and you can see his hand and arm as well. I will zoom in closer in the next photo.

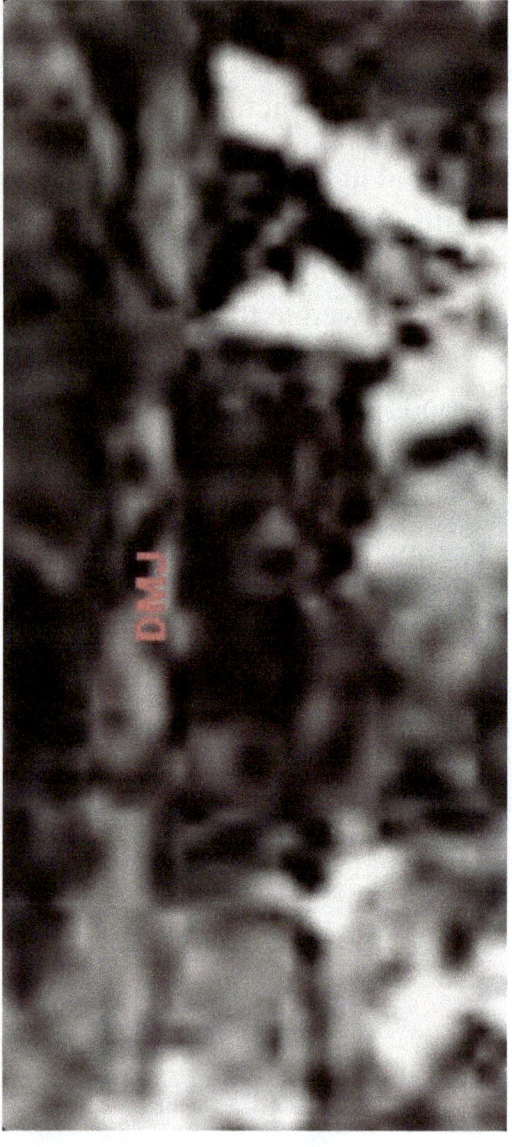

Yes, it's blurry. It's zoomed in like 1000 times but there he is.

This is f or reference for those who need help seeing him.

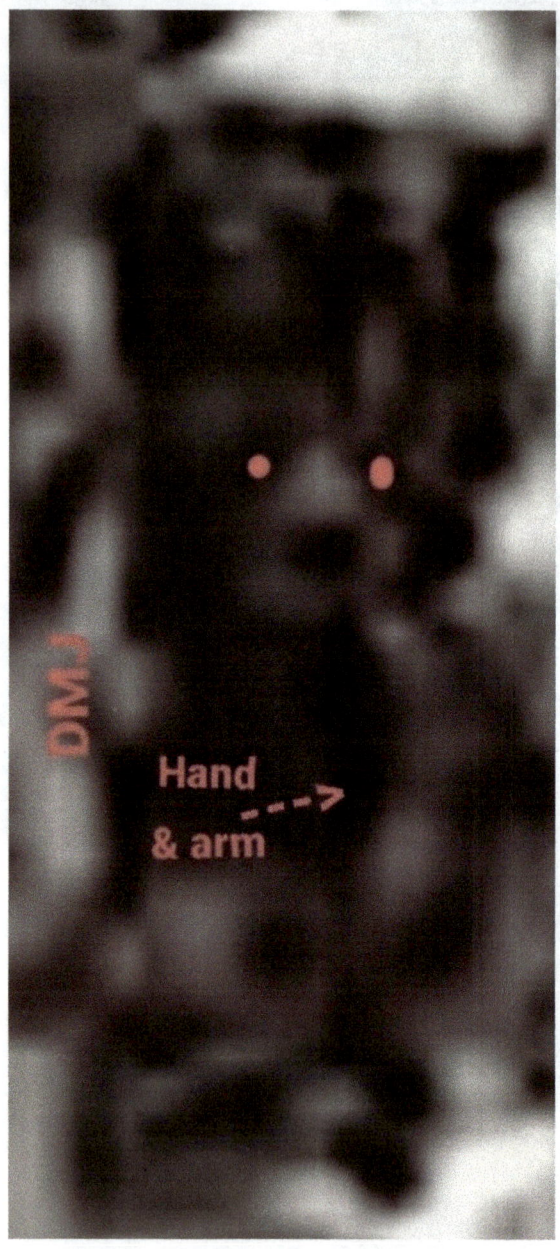

I easily recognize him by his "droopy" eyes. He is the only one that I have encountered that has this appearance. As a matter of fact, they all look different. They each have different characteristics about their appearance just as we do.

Again, just recently, Aubree and I visited the same spot in the back yard. A possible stick glyph caught both of our eyes. We stopped to look around. It seemed to be pointing towards the woods. There was a tree snapped over in there and we kept hearing knocks and whistles etc. So, I asked if I could take some pictures and said I'd love to see you if you don't mind. The following are the pictures I took. Notice

the possible stick glyph on the ground at the bottom of this photo. It seems to be an "arrow" pointing to the woods.

Close up of the possible glyph.

Next, I will show a photo I took after asking permission. This is the area where we heard tree knocks and whistles. The subject I saw after zooming in is on the far left.

Here is the zoomed in and cropped portion of the previous

photo. Do you see him or her?

Zoomed in closer. Now can you see him or her?

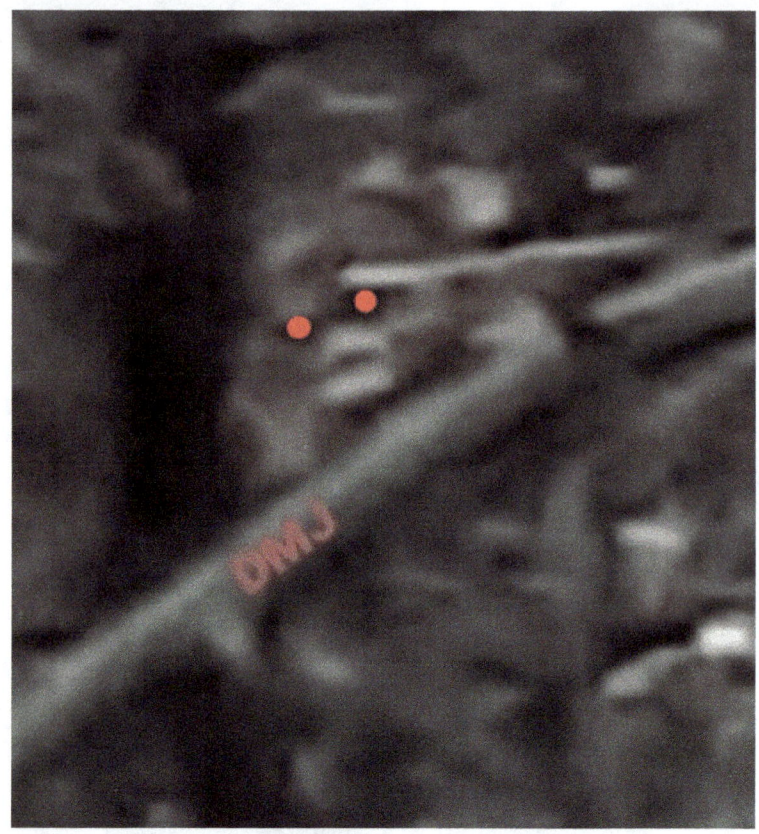

Eyes dotted by me for reference

It is comforting to know they are always close by. Anytime I have the opportunity, I go to the woods here at home and talk with them.

Speaking of talking with them, I have one more short story to share with you. One day my little dog was very sick. All day long, he kept vomiting, and he had bloody diarrhea. He wasn't able to eat or even drink water. He could barely even get up and walk. I had no idea what was wrong with him, but I had the feeling he would not make it through the night. I could not get into to see the vet because it was on a Sunday.

I have been told by a few different people that the bigfoot possess the ability to heal. It has something to do with their vibration when they lay their hands on you. I was desperate and as I sat there with my dog on the porch, I asked out loud to my Friends if there was anything at all that they could do for him. I asked them if they could, please help him. I told them he was very sick, and I could not get him in to see the doctor. I told them how special he was to me, and I didn't want him to die.

I sadly went to bed that night not expecting to find him alive in the morning. I woke the next morning and to my astonishment, he was up jumping around and wagging his tail like there had never been anything wrong with him at all! He was eating, drinking, and playing. As a matter of fact, he looked better than I have seen him in many years. He is pretty old and doesn't get around too well. But there he was acting like a puppy again. I thanked my Friends profusely for helping him. I was so happy!

It seems that whenever you are down and feel like you don't have a friend in the world, they are always there. They do care about those who take the time to get acquainted with them. They are not like most people. They genuinely care for us. For the most part, people are too busy with the cares of this world, and they look out for number one. But it has been my experience that the bigfoot show unconditional love for each other and for all of God's creation.

So next time you are out there taking a walk in the woods, just speak with them. Even if you don't see anything, know that they see you. They are never far from us.

Chapter 26
Seeing Is Believing

This chapter is dedicated to the 2 bigfoot friends who revealed themselves to me at my now research area that I call Stone Doll Holler. As a matter of fact, this encounter is WHY it is now my research area. They opened my eyes completely so that I could plainly see that there was no more question of their existence. Never again has a twinkling of doubt entered my mind. I saw them clearly with my own 2 eyes. Not camouflaged. They wanted me to see them. They had a purpose and a reason for doing this. Let me explain...

The day was July 15th, 2020. Eric and I had decided to go to a very cold body of water that is deep in the forest. It isn't extremely well known by the general public and is most often free of visitors. The water at this spot is fed by a spring and has a beautiful waterfall down the side of a large bluff. The water here is clear and very cold. A wonderful place to cool off on a hot summer day and it was 107 degrees on this day.

The road leading down to this area cuts off from the main gravel road onto a side road. It is a long, winding descent down the mountain on a narrow one lane, gravel road. At the bottom it is a dead end. You must drive slowly because of all the potholes and big rocks. As we drove along, we noticed quite a few tree structures in this deep wooded area. There were many of them on both sides of the road. As far as you can see, all around you are thick woods and ferns growing along the sides of this road. It is a beautiful place looking like a totally different world as you descend down this mountain.

As we descended farther down the mountain, we finally came to the bottom of the holler to an open area that is atop a steep embankment that leads down to the water and a gravel bar. We got out of our truck and Eric, as usual, took off to the water to explore and left me up by the truck alone. I had an odd, eerie feeling as I stood there. Then I heard what I interpreted to be a low growl of some sort from off in the thick tree line. I just shrugged it off thinking it was probably my imagination.

I walked down towards the water and found Eric there walking around on the bank. As we stood there, we started to hear very strange noises. What I can only describe as sounding like a mother turkey calling for her young. We heard this quite a few times and then we heard what sounded sort of like a bull frog croaking. All of this noise was coming from a particular direction in a certain area. Eric walked down the bank to look around. Then, I spotted something moving in the trees along the rocky embankment. It was a dark figure watching us and continuing to make this strange turkey noise. I yelled for Eric to come and see, but before he got to me, it was gone. So again, Eric went on his way exploring the area as I stood in the same spot. I didn't see it anymore, so I thought I would go ahead and start taking a video of the beautiful scenery and documenting our day as I normally do when we go out.

As soon as I turned on my camera, I saw that our observer had returned to the same spot that it was earlier. It was crouching down beside a large tree behind some brush about 30 feet from me. Eric, at this time, was down by the waterline right below where it was crouched. I started yelling at him that it had returned. I continued to film. Because Eric did not see what I saw the first time, he had no fear and thought maybe I had just imagined I had seen something. He walked along the water with this "creature" just above him, watching his every move. As I continued filming the creature, it sat motionless except for an occasional movement which told me it was still there. I tried to be as calm as I could. This dark figure wasn't like anything I had ever seen before. It was big! Is this what we had been searching for all of these years? I have to admit, I was a bit scared, but I tried to keep my composure and continued to film.

As I watched this dark figure, I realized something. We are trapped at the end of a dead-end road and the only thing behind us was a very tall bluff. It was an inescapable point. There was nowhere to go. The only way out was to walk back up the steep embankment, directly towards this creature. I got a dreadful, gut wrenching feeling that if we were going to make it out of here, we were going to have to walk right by it to get to our truck and to safety.

I started to feel very uncomfortable, and I told Eric I wanted to leave. I turned the camera off after about 2 minutes of filming and just told myself to walk as swiftly as I could without running and to look straight ahead. Do not look over to the side. Keep your eyes focused forward and trudge on until you see the truck. As we walked, I said out loud "We are your friends. We didn't mean to disturb you. Please forgive us. We will leave you at peace now."

We finally made it out of there. It seemed like an eternity walking up the steep embankment and I was never so relieved to reach the truck. But little did I know what all I had caught on that video. That is something I wouldn't find out for a few days...what we saw on the film is what amazed us the most!

I uploaded my video to Facebook as I normally do to show my friends what happened to us that day. One of my friends messaged me the next day and had taken a screenshot from my video. It showed a large face. He put it in black and white to show the details better. I was amazed!

Can you see the big one beside the tree? His head and face are visible. I have circled the big guy's head. Little did I know

there was another white bigfoot behind him.

We will take a closer look next.

Closer and in color.

There was also a white one to the right that raised up slowly in the video the ducked down ever so slowly using the wind blowing the foilage as cover for their movement.

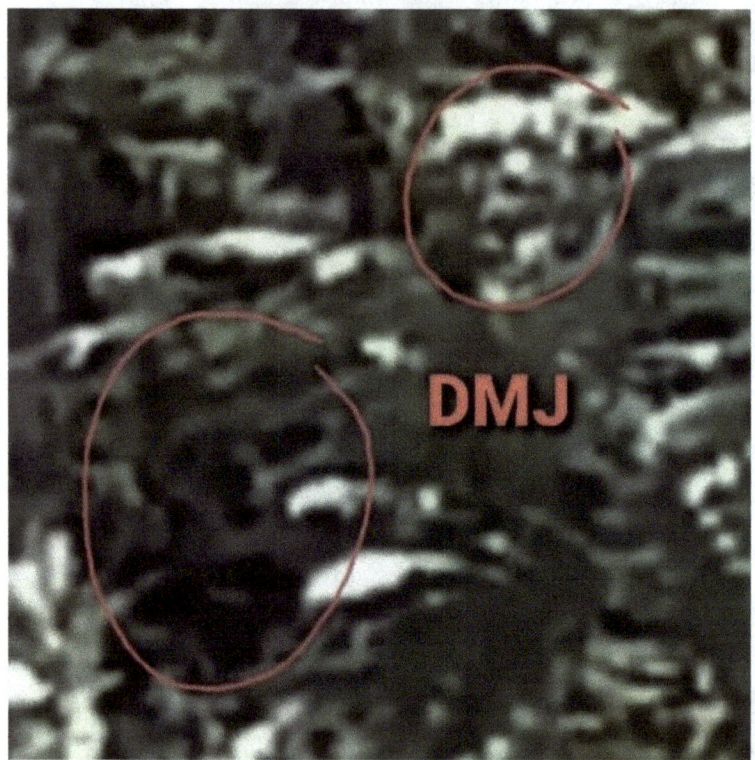

Of course, this isn't crystal clear. It is a screenshot from a moving video and is zoomed in ALOT. But this totally changed my entire way of thinking and looking at the world and the possibility that there is way more out there than we will probably ever know. Let's get closer…

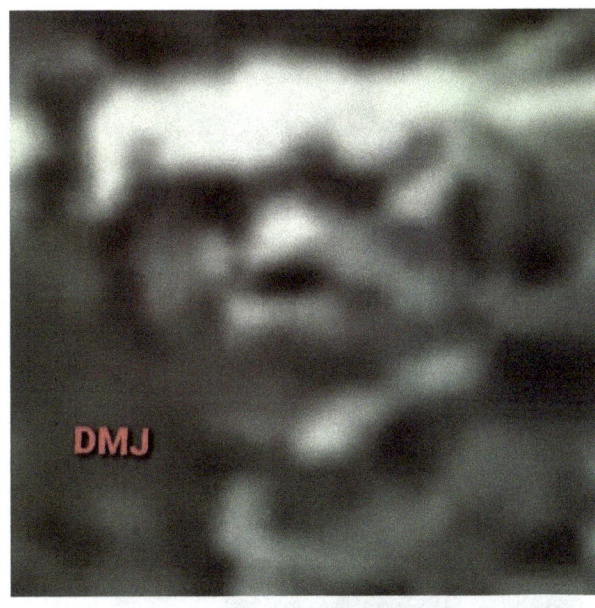
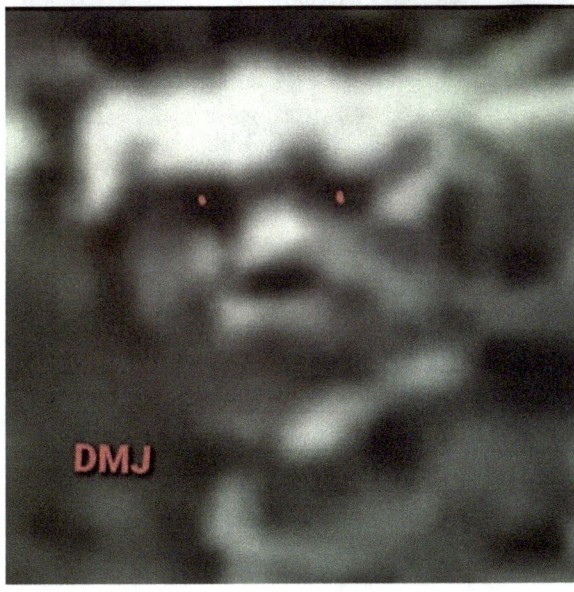

Here is a close up of the white bigfoot being behind the other one as he raised up to peek over the brush at us. I am so glad someone spotted him for me. I had previously overlooked him because of the obvious one that I saw while I was there at the time.

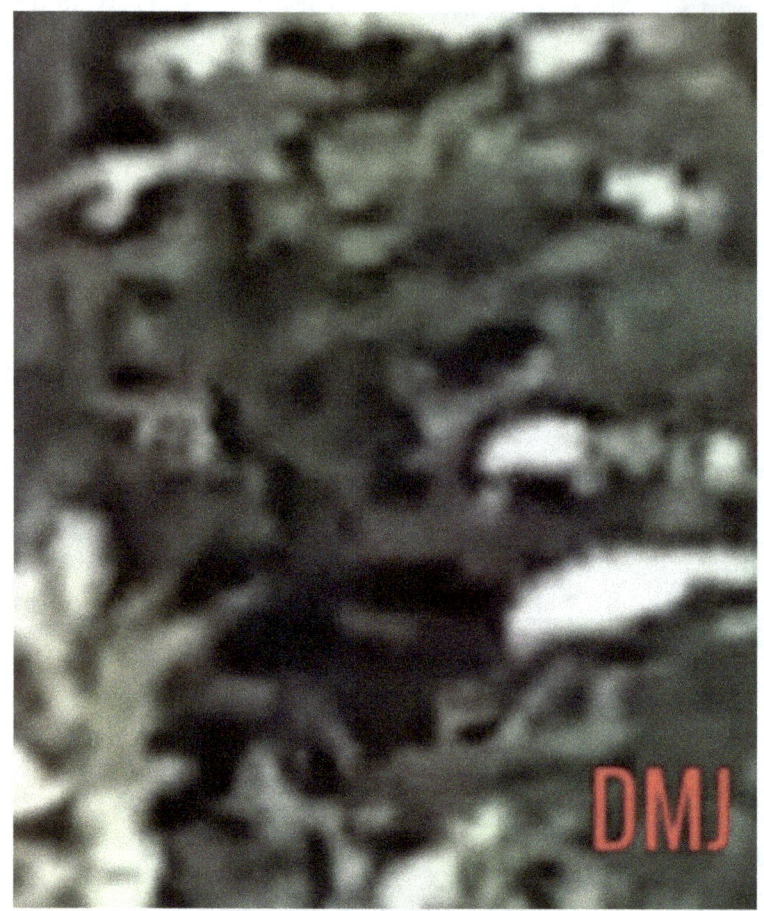

Here is a close up of the big gray one. He has his mouth open slightly. I believe he was panting because it was so hot that day and he needed a drink from the spring we were at. In my original video you can see him licking his lips and he sticks his tongue out. His tongue was gray as well.

Eyes dotted by me for reference

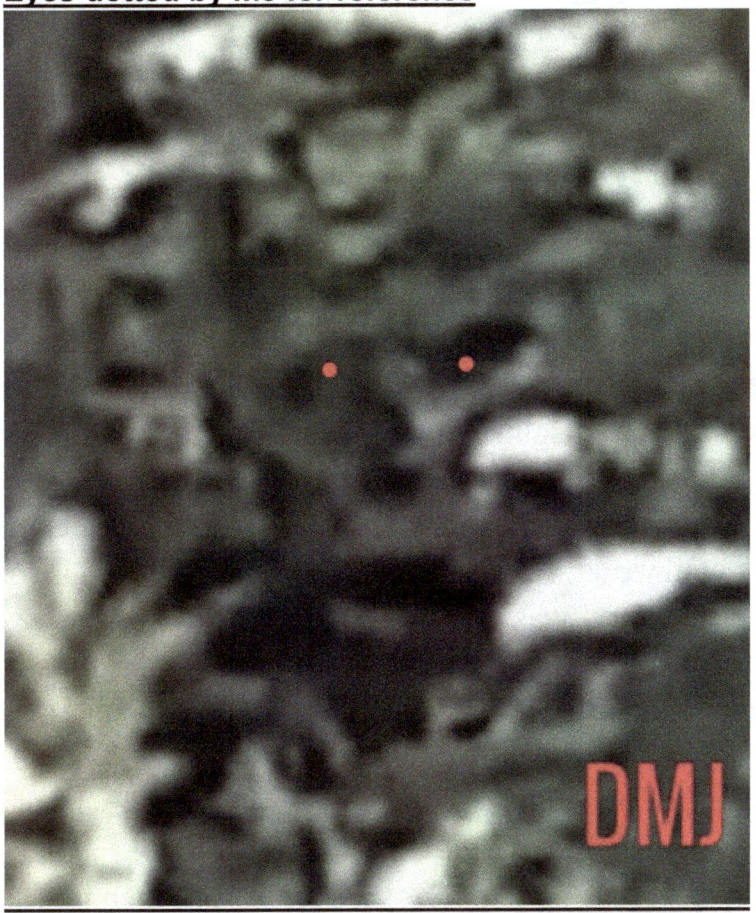

About two days later, after posting my video on Facebook, another friend messaged me saying what I had on that film was astonishing. In the original video, you can see that there is "something" crouching there beside that tree but not a lot of detail. My friend zoomed in to get a closer look. Lo and behold, you can see so much detail in the zoomed in version.

It had dark, deep-set eyes and a raised brow ridge and its mouth was in an open position. It looked as if it was panting because of the heat. You could even see that it stuck its tongue out and licked its lips. That is where I got these colored screenshots from.

It sat there almost motionless. Then in the video as I said "That, that guy is watching us", it raised its eyebrows. Immediately after this, the wind blew some foliage in front of its face. As the wind blew the foliage, you could see its hand quickly scratching its chin and all of its fingers and an opposing thumb moving with quick precision. I was amazed how this creature used the wind blowing the leaves around to disguise the movement of its hand. Very intelligent. I also noticed that at another time that it looked to be putting its finger in its mouth. I was totally shocked by the detail we saw in this zoomed in version of my video. Needless to say, I was thrilled with the evidence that was caught on our video. As well as seeing this big grayish colored one, someone else pointed out to me the large white one behind the gray one. It was almost equal in size to the darker one and was standing further back. In the video, you can see it rise up so slowly it was barely noticeable. It rose up to peek over some brush then just as slowly as it rose up, it ducked back down out of sight. We decided it was time to do a little more investigating and planned a return visit. It was time to seek answers as to the size of these bigfoot.

We returned a few days later to examine the tree that the gray one was crouching beside. It was hard for Eric to get to this area because it was steep. He walked through the wooded area as my heart raced in fear of him walking up onto these creatures who may be hiding there still...or again. He finally got to the top of the embankment and there was some very tall grass there. He saw that a large area of the grass had been mashed down as if something had been bedding there. He finally reached the area where the tree was. It was in a dried-up rock bed.

There was nothing there but large boulders to stand on, so he didn't see any footprints. I took photos of Eric standing beside this tree. It was as wide as his shoulders. In the video, the gray bigfoots face was every bit the width of that tree so that makes our bigfoots face approximately 20 inches wide. Here is Eric standing beside that same tree and also the bigfoot beside that tree. Notice the head is basically the same width as the tree. Here I have drawn lines on both sides of the tree and on both sides of the bigfoot's face.

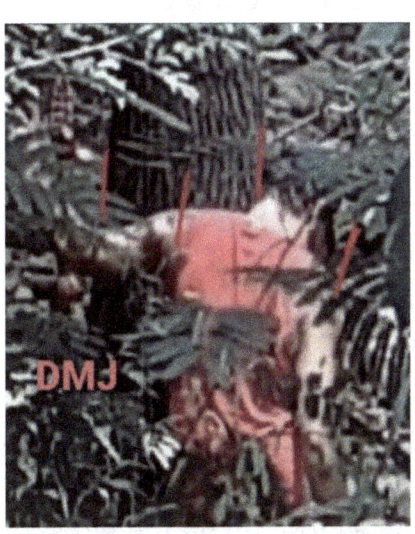 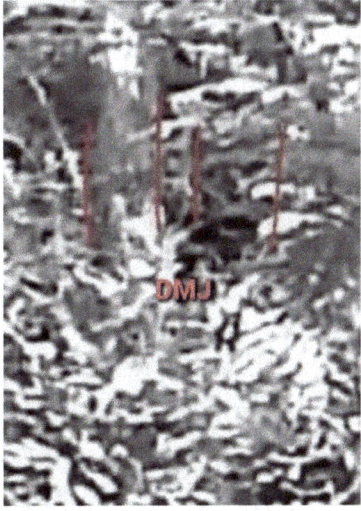

We decided to leave some gifts, so Eric tied an apple up in that tree with a small rope. We also had some kitty toys I had purchased earlier, and he also tied those up in the tree. Then once again we started hearing strange noises. We heard the "turkey call" again and then a "WHOOOO!" from out in the wooded area. We decided it was time to leave. But that was not our last encounter in this spot.

We returned a few days later to check on our gifts. The apple had been taken. Eric had threaded the small rope through the apple to prevent it from simply falling onto the ground. Something had totally removed this apple from this dangling small rope. There were no scraps of it anywhere on the ground to point to any sort of rodent activity. It had simply been removed from the rope. The cat toy was still there, however, it was taken a couple of weeks later.

A few minutes after Eric got back down to the water, I decided to take some photos of the area and another video. As I was filming, once again in that same spot behind that tree, I saw movement! I could see, as I was filming, that something dark was back there. My heart began to pound as I watched and filmed. I could see this creature was ducking and then going behind the tree. It also looked as though there was another dark figure above this one farther back in the woods. After seeing a close up on the video of what had been there the last time watching us, I was not as calm as I was the first time. I did continue to film for a couple of minutes, but my fear got the better of me and I wanted to leave. We started walking up that steep embankment again to get out and all I could think of was how BIG this creature was and how close it was. I tripped and almost fell down. But we made it up to the truck.

Before I got into the truck, I spoke out loud to "them" again reassuring them we meant no harm and I left the only thing I had with me at the time, a Twinkie, on a large rock out there.

These are an incredible, unknown species that have captured my interest and now I know for a FACT that they are real and that they do exist. Any doubt I may have had has been completely erased. As I have furthered my research, these beings seem to be more human like. I believe them to be primal people. They have a language and can also speak and communicate with us in any language. They are well suited to survive and thrive on their own. I will continue on in my research and do everything I can to protect our new Bigfoot friend's privacy. They deserve every bit of respect. If there is one thing you can take away from all of this, it is knowing that the world is a remarkable, adventurous place, full of amazement, if you only open your minds and eyes to it!

Chapter 27

Various captures

In this chapter, I will post an array of different encounters and photos I have captured in various locations. I have so many short stories and encounters that need to be shared. I can't possibly share them all as they are too numerous. But I will wrap it up in this chapter.

Here is a peeker I captured in a photo on a wooded trail when my granddaughter Aubree was with us. She seems to attract them to her. This particular one was watching her as she stood and posed for a picture for me on a very large tree that had fallen across the trail.

Can you see him or her?

Let's look closer…

This appears to be a juvenile that was watching us as we walked by, unbeknownst to us.

Next is a screenshot I took from a video of the area way back behind Dead Mans Mountain. We had never been this far back, and we were finding large footprints there. Unbeknownst to me, we were being watched. I believe this is Urijah. At least it appears to be. He was far back, but I spotted him on the video later on and I took a screenshot of him. Notice his broad shoulders and head that sits directly on them. He has no neck.

Urijah is a very handsome young bigfoot. He was very far away. Approximately 250 feet away and he still appears HUGE. I'm not sure how big he is now but he has grown considerably since he left me those 10-inch footprints. The footprints we were finding were approximately 13-14 inches long which coincides with his tracks now. Next page are the tracks we were finding down there.

Now I will share the incident I referred to in Chapter 17 about the stick glyphs. As I was looking at these intricate glyphs on the ground, I kept hearing rocks clacking together on the bluff in front of me. This bluff is a good 100+ feet tall. I decided to take photos of the area I was hearing these rocks clacking together, and I'm glad I did! Now, I know you can't see the individual up there in this photo, but this is to

give you an idea of the area and how far they are from me. I was zoomed in as close as I could when taking this photograph. I will zoom in and crop the culprit out in the next photo. Now you can see what I'm dealing with most of the time. The photos are taken from such a distance that when I zoom in to get a better look, it is so pixelated that it is very hard to see. But I do still try. Most of the photos I have are from a very far distance. It is very hard and very rare to get a clear photo of them but let's look closer…

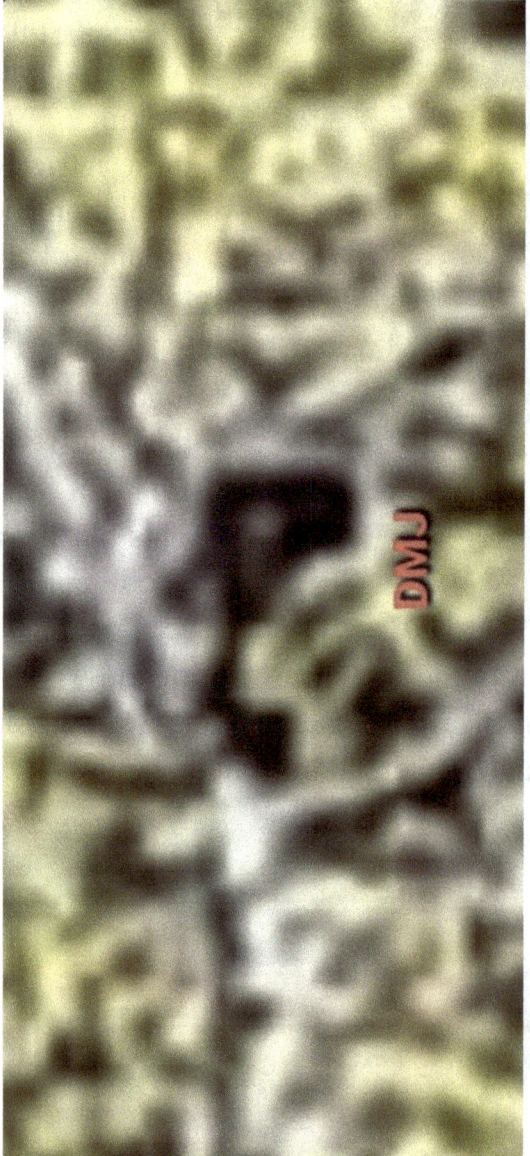

He is up there watching us. His head is visible in the center of this photo. I see a prominent brow ridge, eyes, and nose.

Why is he clacking rocks together? We may never know. Maybe alerting others in the area that I was finding and photographing the stick glyphs. Maybe to say hello? I do not know.

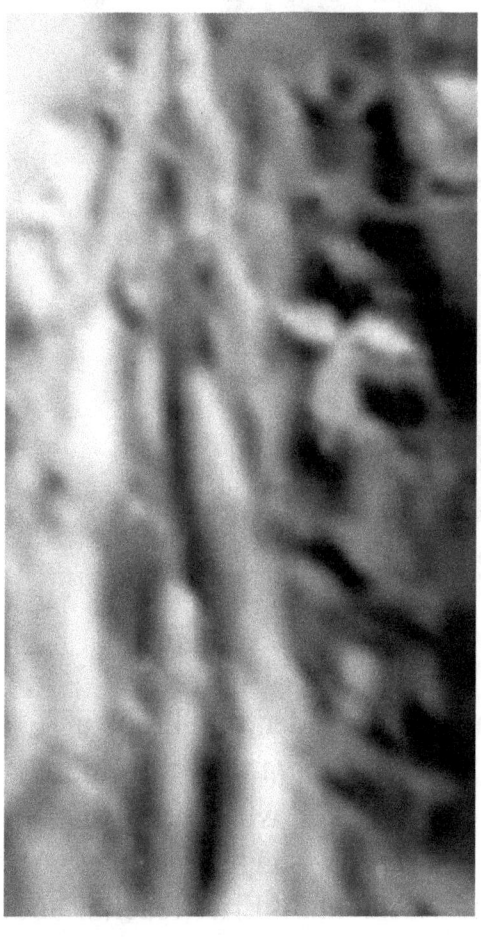

Next, I will show you a screenshot that my friend Cindy took from one of my videos. I was in my back yard filming after I spotted one of my Friends back there. She has a very good eye. Here is one of my friends peeking around a tree at me. See the right side of the photo. You can clearly see his face. His eye and nose and mouth. I LOVE this capture and will always be indebted to Cindy for spotting him for me. This one is hanging on my "wall of memories", and I cherish it!

Next, I have a screenshot from a video that I took at Stone Doll Holler. My friend Ta'mara took it from my video and sent to me. I was shocked when I saw this one! You can see their eyes and their V-shaped hairlines. And they appear to be around 7.5 feet tall. Erics reach is about

7.5 feet when he reaches above his head. And their heads are about the same height as Erics hand.

Eric had a tape measure, and he was measuring the height and width of another giant that had been spotted on another video I took at this same spot. As he measured, I guided him as to where to hold the tape measure according to the screen shot that I had received of the giant from a friend on Facebook. Little did we know these two big guys were standing right behind him. They made no noise and did not alert us that they were even there. And while we were there, we saw absolutely nothing! This is yet another example of their ability to hide in plain sight. Only with the help of a camera lens were they visible.

As I was previously speaking about, I had received another screenshot from a facebook friend that they had taken from another video. It shows a GIANT something. It has an appearance sort of like a gorilla and it appears to be sitting down back there where I was filming. The reason I was filming in that direction was because as I walked to the gifting tree, Eric spotted something about 7 foot tall and jet-black running towards me. There is also a white being on the right side of the picture peeking around the bushes at me. Here is that screen shot. Can you see the gorilla looking being sitting there with his hand up by his mouth? And to the right of him is a white being with what looks like doggy ears. Next, I will dot the eyes for you for reference.

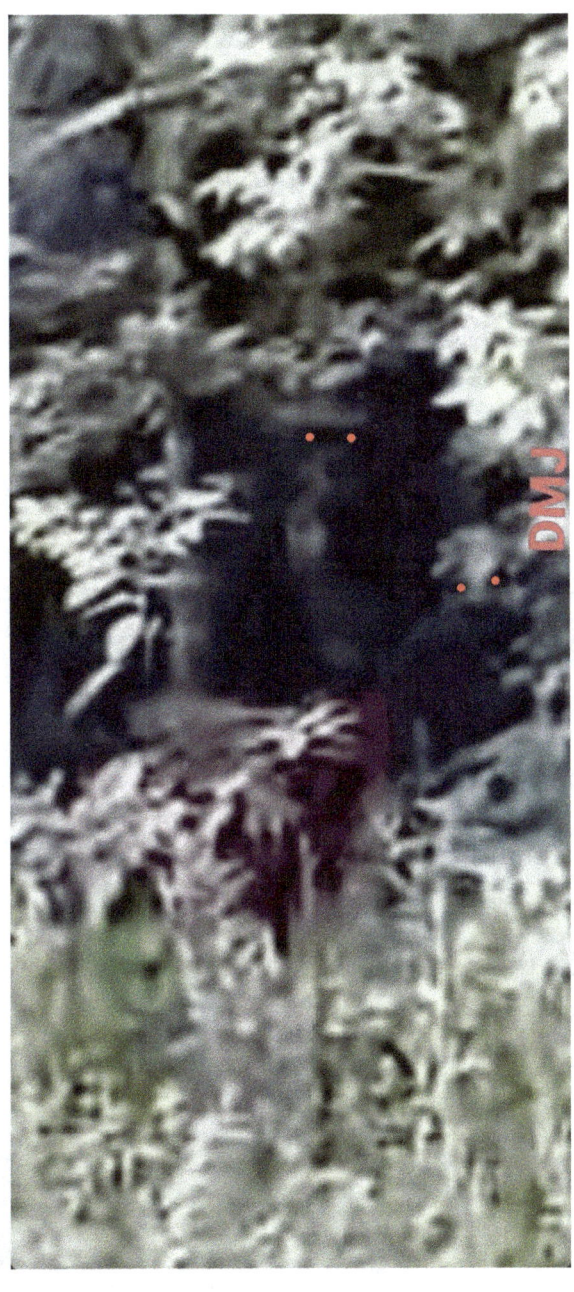

These beings can control what we see with our eyes and/or what we can only see through the camera lens. This is another example of that fact and may explain why they do not like our cameras. They avoid trail cameras I have put out and I learned not to do that anymore. It actually made them leave and I believe they did not trust me anymore. It took a long time to regain any sort of trust and communication with them. That happened at the beginning of my research many years ago. Never again! Now I ask for permission to use my camera when I'm out there.

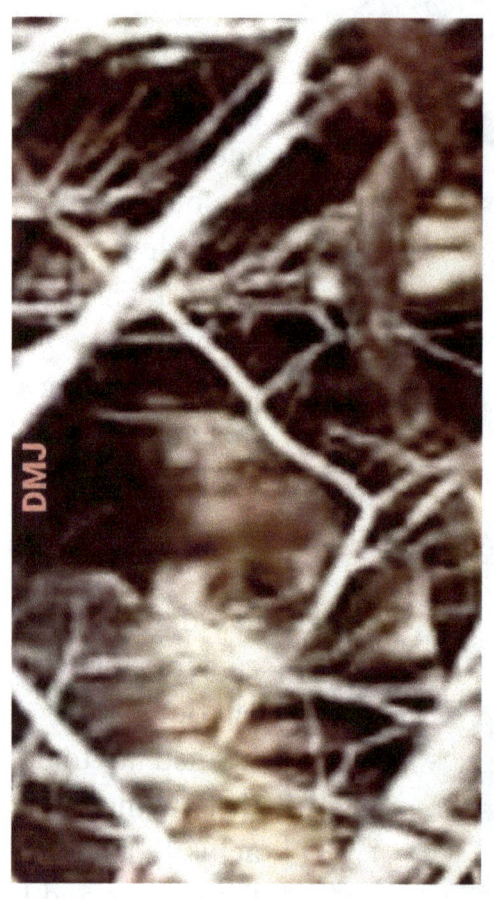

Now, I will show you a photo I snapped while we were walking a trail deep in the wilderness. The population of the nearest town is 9. And there are no other towns within 20+ miles from there. This is a zoomed in portion of that photograph. Can you see him peeking through the bushes at us? This one has a sort of chimpanzee appearance to him. There are so many different beings out there. Each one I show you looks different. I have come to realize that there is more than just Bigfoot out there. Next, I will dot his eyes for reference for those who have a hard time seeing…

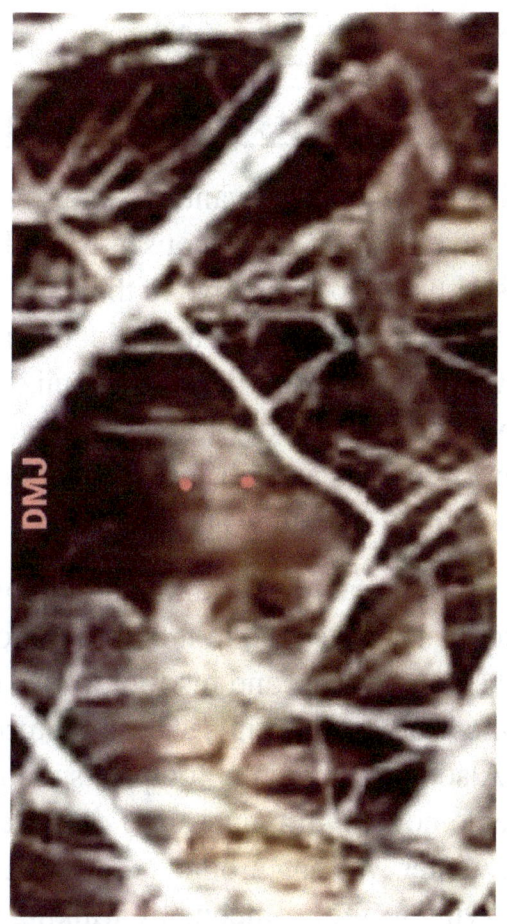

I could go on and on. I have so many photos to share and so many things to show you that one book couldn't contain it all. Maybe some day I will write another book. There is so much I want to share with you.

Chapter 28

Footprints In The Sand

Finally in this last chapter, I want to share some footprints I have found. I have thousands of photos of footprints, so I had to be selective in the ones I share. I have some very large footprints and a lot of juvenile footprints. Urijah's footprint is very recognizable to me as I have followed him for over 3 years. Some are Eden's and some are Timothys as well. And some, the larger ones, I do not know who they are. So here we go.

I will show you the trackway we found in February 2020. Eric had accidentally stepped in it before I photographed it. He weighs 210 pounds, and his footprint is not nearly as deep as these other footprints. These footprints are very deep. Also notice how the footprints are in a straight line. People do not walk in this way. I don't see someone out there in winter walking around barefooted to the ice-cold water trying to fool someone by walking in a straight line. Whatever left those prints was heavy. And the strangest thing was when I returned the next morning, not one single footprint was there. All had been erased. There wasn't even one single footprint there. I believe

they saw us looking at them and "cleaned up their mess" so to speak. And I have since learned this was Urijah's footprints.

A long trackway going down to the freezing water then it returned and came back up to the trees and disappeared.

Next, I will share a few more close up shots of his foot.

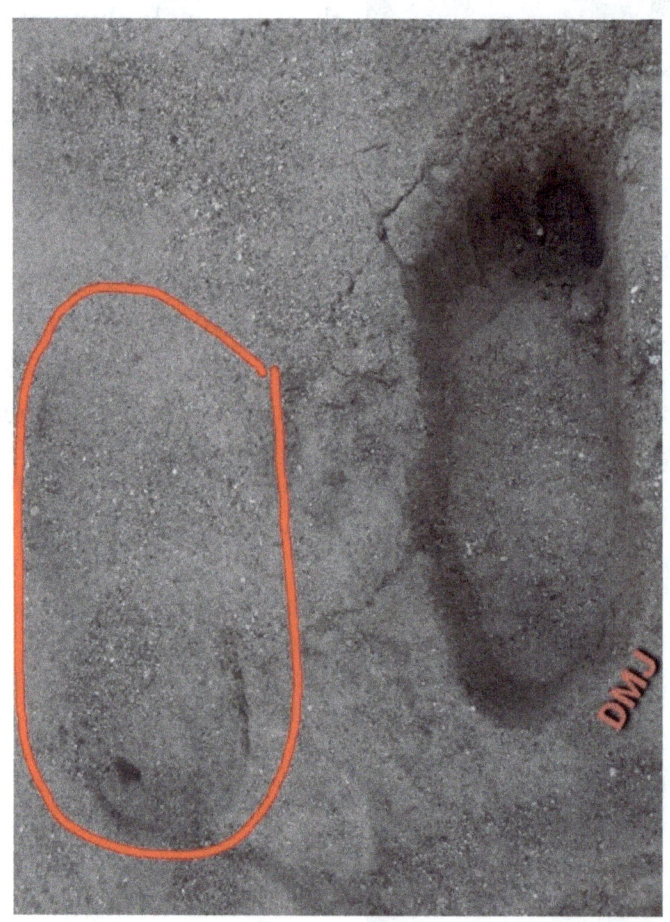

Here is one shot and I have circled where I stepped. My shoe print is barely visible. Notice how deep the bigfoots track is. The ground was frozen hard and would not give an inch. Imagine the weight of what left this track! Also notice the elongated heel and the placement of the ankle is farther up than on a human. The placement of the ankle gives the individual the ability to carry more weight. This is not a human trait. Also, the ankle bone is clearly seen here as a bulge on the side of the foot. People's tracks don't show this. Here is another good view of his foot:

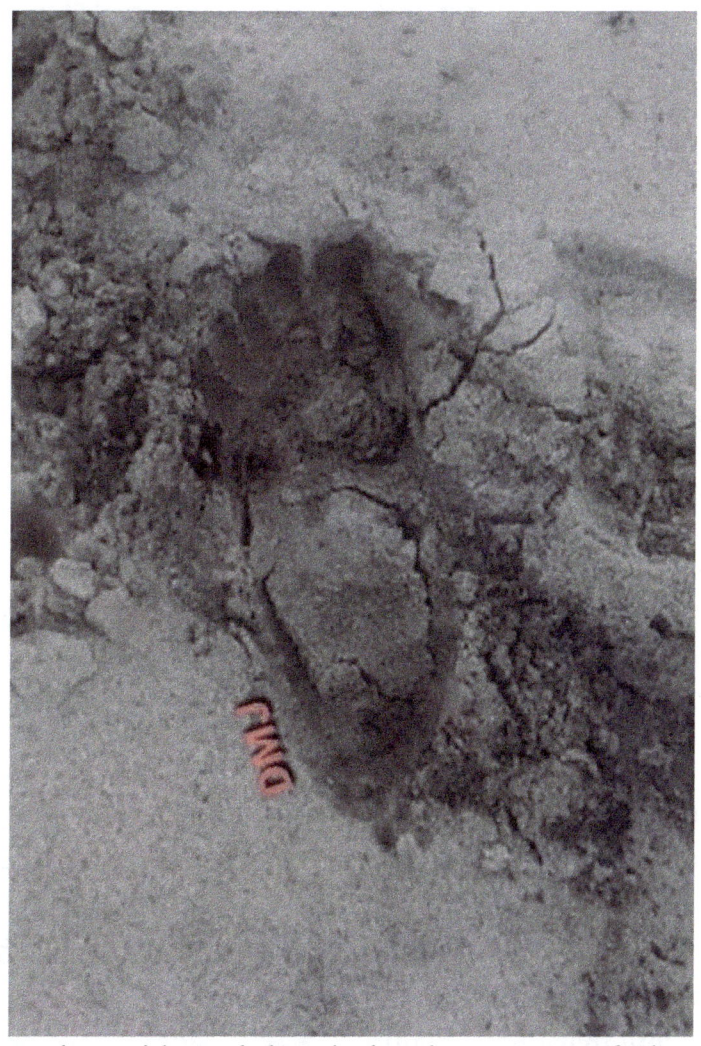

Notice the midtarsal break in the center of the foot. Humans do not have this trait. Their foot bends in the center. It is clearly seen here and in these photos. You can see how his foot "folds" in the center.

He also has very long toes and I have a few casts of his footprints. I can now recognize his footprint when I see it. It is very familiar to me after all of these years.

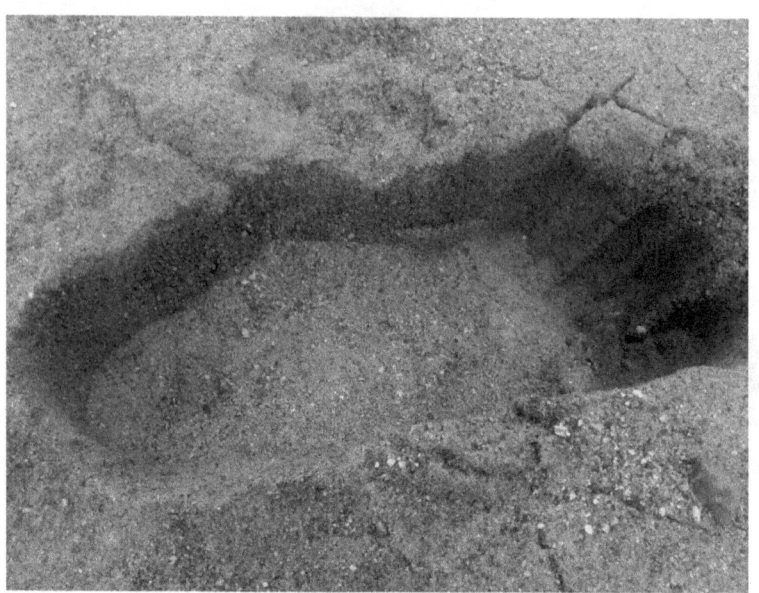

Urijah was a juvenile when he left these tracks. They only measured between 10 and 11 inches long at that time. Now his foot is around 13 to 14 inches long.

I have also found larger footprints as well. I will share a few of them with you. Keep in mind, a lot of these are found in the winter months. Also keep in mind that my shoe is almost exactly 10 inches long (9 7/8"). A lot of the time I fail to have a tape measure with me when I encounter them. So, I use my shoe for scale. Here are a select few that I have found:

This one is approximately 13 inches long. This one is not Urijah or any of the other "regulars" that I see. I find many tracks in my research areas.

This one is approximately 15 inches long by 7 inches wide.

The ground was frozen. Here is the next consecutive step. We have a left and a right foot.

Now I will show you what appears to be a deformed footprint. It appears that this individual may have suffered a bad injury.

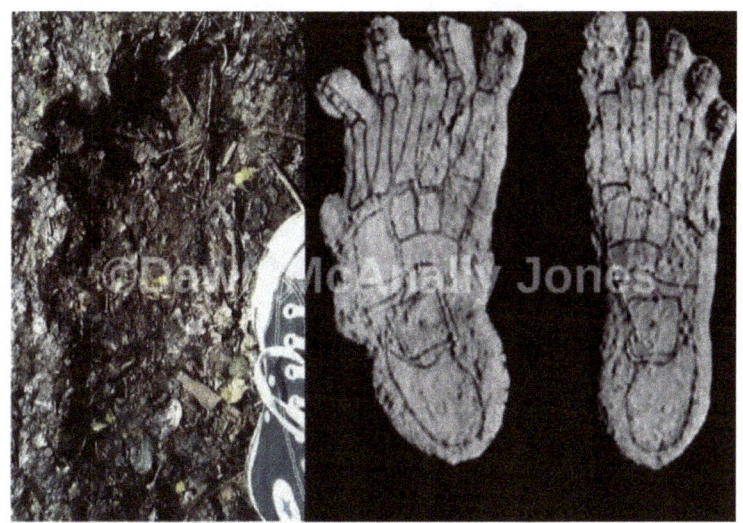

I later watched a documentary that had Dr. Grover Krantz in it. The print I found reminded me of the crippled Sasquatch print he found back in the 1960's. He took casts of it and drew in the bones on the casts showing the injury. I took a photo of the one I found and used my shoe for scale. Since my shoe is almost exactly 10 inches long, this print was approximately 16 inches long. I found this track before I started using a tape measure. Anyway, my sasquatch print injury (left side) is almost identical to his footprint cast injury (right side) except that the heels are going in different directions. I wonder what caused the injury or if it's a common deformity.

Whatever left the footprint was massive and heavy. I can say that.

Next is an example of the juveniles I find here at my research areas all the time. It seems they like to come out and play at night. Especially in the winter. The cold

doesn't seem to affect them at all. They even get into the water in January and walk around as these next photos show. These appear to be Urijah's.

Who would be out there walking around barefooted in freezing cold water in January?

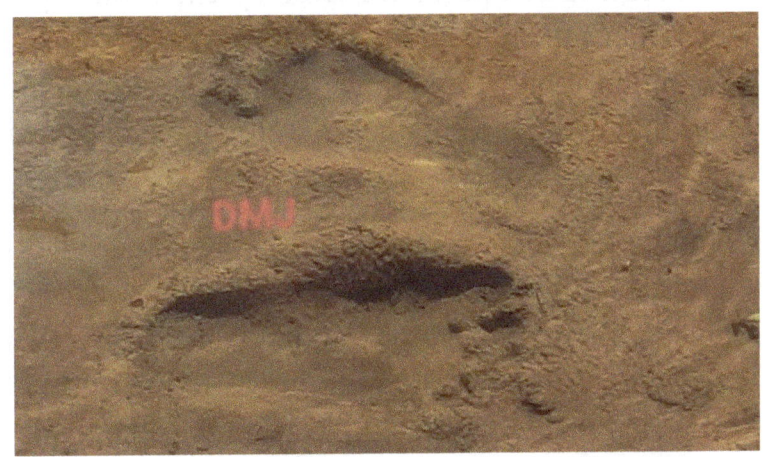

At times there is also the question of "Why is there only one footprint?" I hear this all the time. But it seems to

happen to me a lot. Many times, I do only find a single print. How is that possible? Do they enter into a portal which takes them to another realm? Are they interdimensional? Sometimes, the tracks stop suddenly. Does that mean the creature or animal just disappeared?

Many oddities are interwoven in the subject of Bigfoot. Some researchers are continuously encountering things that seem unlikely or impossible. Things they refuse to accept. Others have slowly embraced this side of Bigfoot. The strange side, which is leading us to the truth. I have concluded that Bigfoot and the spirit world may be more alike than we thought. After all that I have seen and experienced in my lifetime, this is not a far stretch of the imagination for me. Open your minds to that possibility.

In the end, the mystery of finding a single Bigfoot footprint remains just that. A mystery. It continues to fascinate both believers and skeptics. Whether they are intentionally deceiving us, or it is just the mysterious abilities that they possess, the truth behind these single prints remains unknown. So, keep searching. Who knows? You may be the one to finally uncover the secrets of Bigfoot.

If you do happen to find a Bigfoot track, know that it is a gift. Sometimes literally intentional. At times I have asked for a footprint and the next day, I discover they have obliged me of my request.

I am going to wrap this up now. I have laid all this out for you to ponder and hopefully learn a few things from.

My goal is to teach others and raise awareness of the truth. That what we as humans think we know as a "superior race" is not all that is out there. There is more…

There is so much more!

Thank you for reading.

Acknowledgements

I would like to thank the following people in no particular order for their contributions and assistance in helping this book to become a reality. Some of whom are family members who allowed me to share their encounters. Others are good friends who are accomplished authors, and some are well-known Bigfoot researchers.

Amber Weaver

My daughter who has lived through and continues to live through a lot of the strangeness along beside me. We are two peas in a pod. We have even shared the same "psychic" dreams (or visions from another time and place) and are connected in a way most people could not comprehend.

Clayton Anderson

My son, who has also experienced many of the things I have written about in this book. We share a common ground and understanding of the paranormal side of life as we know it. After all, we have lived through it and experienced many of these "unbelievable" things while together.

Aubree Weaver

My youngest granddaughter who is my "partner in crime." She is always eager to accompany me to the woods and to learn more about the People of the Forest. She has now taught me many things by being so observant. Many things which I would have overlooked if not for her keen eye. The Forest People seem to love her by always showing up when she is around. She will be an excellent Bigfoot Huntress some day!

Michelle Weaver

My oldest granddaughter loves to accompany us to the woods and learn more about nature and try new things. She is always eager to learn and experiment to see what the Forest People enjoy and do for us.

Igor Burtsev

My friend and leading bigfoot researcher who currently lives in Moscow, Russia. Author of many books including the bestseller **Bigfoot Explorers and Introduction to Hominology.** Thank you for all your support, guidance, educated opinion and input into my findings. You have been a huge inspiration for me.

Carter Buschardt

My friend and the author of many exhilarating books including **Sasquatch Evidence of an Enigma I, II, and III.** Your books are a wealth of knowledge. Your firsthand experiences involving many epic witnesses and investigations are fascinating. I have learned so much from reading your books and from our conversations. Thank you for your guidance on the how to's of publishing and the use of the Word and Publisher programs. You took the time to call me and guide me through some very confusing times including the process of self-publishing and getting all the legalities taken care of. I truly appreciate it!

Thom Cantrall

An accomplished author of many books and my dear friend. You have been my mentor and cheered me on from day one. You have guided me in everything and taught me so much including how to cast footprints. Thank you for inspiring me to write my own book by publishing my written encounter in your book **Sasquatch Face to Face**. Your generous offer of time to teach others does not go unnoticed nor unappreciated.

Dr. Matthew A. Johnson

A Licensed Clinical Psychologist, a leading bigfoot researcher and author of his own books including **Positive Parenting with a Plan (Grades K-12): FAMILY Rules** and **Bigfoot- A Fifty-Year Journey Come Full Circle (with a foreward by Bob Gimlin)** and **The Xanue- Befriending the Bigfoot Forest People.** You have been a great inspiration and support for me. Your advice and encouragement have been priceless gifts to me.

Tobe Johnson

You have guided me through many odd things I have found including a step-by-step tutorial on how to lift large fingerprints off of my windows at home etc. The Host and Producer of **A Flash of Beauty: The Podcast.** The Co-Producer at **Resonance Productions.** And author at **Hangar 1 Publishing** just to name a few. Thank you for your help on my journey. Your advice has been so helpful on many occasions.

David T. Hollis

You have been a huge support for me through the years. An accomplished author of his own books including **The Mystery of the Iatt Lake Monster-Revealed** and **Squatchland II- Under the Sign of the Crooked Snake.** You have taught me how to spot the bigfoot in my photos and videos when they were so camouflaged that it was almost impossible to see them. You have been a wonderful friend and mentor to me. Thank you for all your support over the years.

A host of friends who have supported me through it all and some who have helped me to see things I would have missed in numerous videos and photos. Some of which I have included here in this book.

Including but in no particular order:

Janice Carter, Craig Woolheater, Jill Remensnyder, Marc Abell, Shane Carpenter, Andrea Billups, Linda Eastburn, Greg Yost, Dan A. Nedrelo, Cindy Larot, Lori Vogel, Nancy Swecker, Ta'mara Wilson, William Morris, Kerry-Ann O'Meara, Michaael Fragosso, C.R. Gay, Deana Loulos, Carl L. Johnson, Darrell Denton, J.R. Noell, Brynn MaGillivray, Cindy Ann Bueno Goodbrake, Yvette Wilborn, Dorraine Fisher, Barb Horn Hartman, Laura Peterson, Elizabeth Post, William Mahaffey, Marsha Dorgan, Diane Marie, Patricia Garrison, Sharon Buck, Ronnie Cates, Renee Wilson, Bobby Boncore, Ana Herrera, Robert Bob Lilibridge, Geddes Gregory, Richard

Norton, Becky Bates, Kelly Gonsalves and many, MANY others that are too numerous to mention!

Bigfoot And Beyond
Life Through The Eyes Of An Intuitive

Copyright Page: ISBN# 978-1-66640-781-5

Copyright 2024. All materials in this book are copyright protected and use and or reproduction are strictly prohibited unless there is explicit permission in writing. All photos are property of Dawn McAnally Jones unless specified otherwise.

Cover image by: Dawn McAnally Jones © Copyright protected.

Printed by Diggy Pod Inc. USA 2024

www.ingramcontent.com/pod-product-compliance
Lightning Source LLC
Chambersburg PA
CBHW050550170426
43201CB00011B/1645